Contents

Contents	1
Features	2
Passage Titles and Levels Chart	4
Series Scope and Sequence Chart	5

Lesson 1
Whistle Like a Bird 6

Lesson 2
Benny's School Trip 10

Lesson 3
I Can Be Anything 15

Lesson 4
A Penny Changes the Day 20

Lesson 5
Nana's Kitchen 25

Lesson 6
The Around-the-World Lunch 30

Lesson 7
The Missing Pet 35

Lesson 8
A Gift to Share 41

Lesson 9
My Prairie Summer 47

Lesson 10
Milo's Great Invention 55

Lesson 11
The School Mural 62

Lesson 12
Diary of a Pioneer Boy 70

Lesson 13
The Grand Canyon Doesn't Scare Me 79

Graphic Organizers
Cause and Effect Chart	88
Character Change Story Map	89
Character Traits Web	90
Story Events Map	91
Compare and Contrast Chart	92
Cluster Story Map	93
Answer Key	94

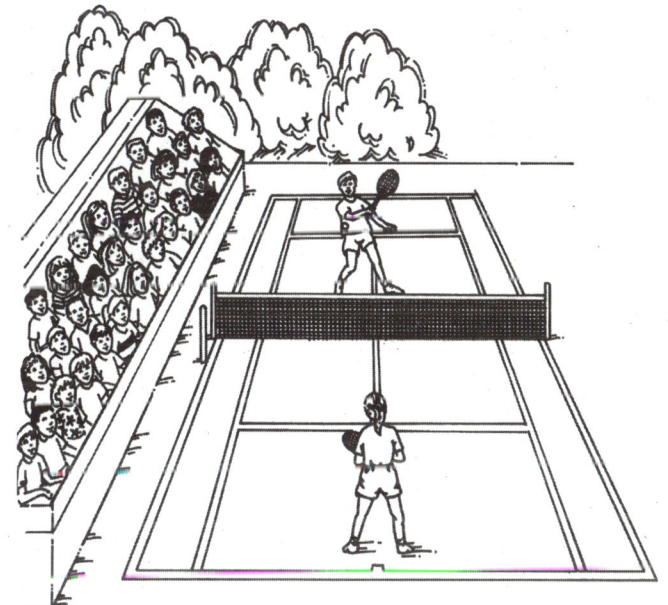

Features

The *Leveled Reading* series uses a variety of carefully leveled passages within a specific genre to supplement learning. In this way, the needs of the variety of readers in the classroom are met.

The high-interest passages within the series may be used for whole group or small group instruction as well as for independent practice. If used for independent practice, passages should be selected at the student's independent reading level to ensure success. For instances where the student will receive direct support, the passages should be at the student's instructional level. It is important that the key vocabulary within passages be overviewed with the student and that the student be encouraged to utilize strategies for understanding new and unfamiliar words.

Each book within the series is divided into lessons. The lessons follow a similar format to help improve the student's reading, fluency, comprehension, vocabulary, and critical thinking. Each lesson includes a leveled passage, Reading Comprehension Check, Vocabulary Practice, and Critical Thinking Activity.

Leveled passages open with a **Get Ready to Read** section that connects the student to the text. The student should read the passage once for pleasure and then a second time for understanding, noting the boldface vocabulary words. The student may write brief summaries or comments about the text in the margins to document his or her understanding of the text. The student should additionally read sections of the text aloud to continue to build his or her fluency skills.

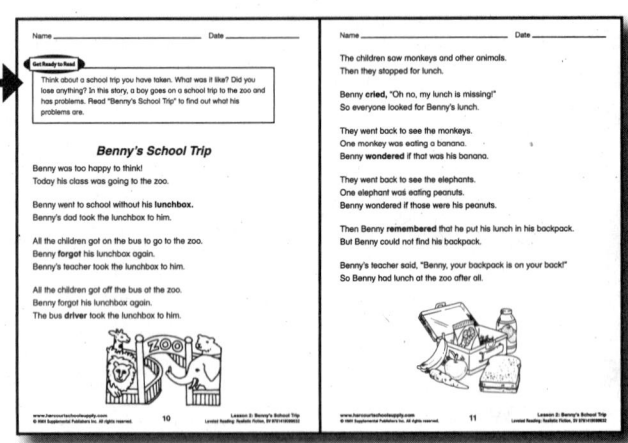

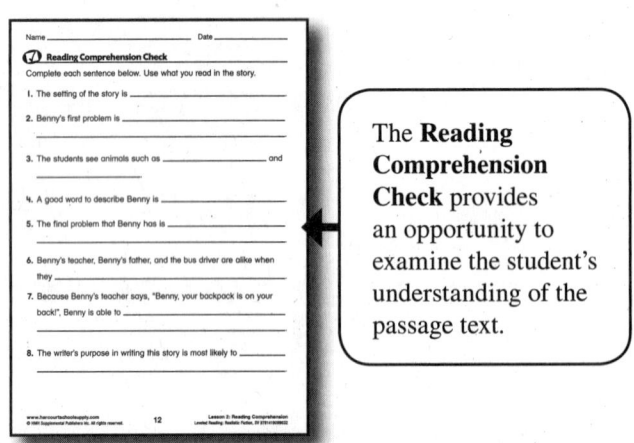

The **Reading Comprehension Check** provides an opportunity to examine the student's understanding of the passage text.

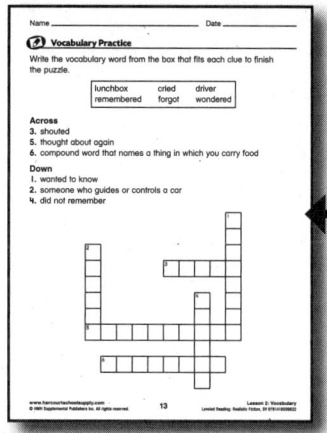

The **Vocabulary Practice** page allows the student to practice his or her knowledge of the key words from the passage. In addition, most vocabulary pages include a **Vocabulary Extension**, where the student may apply higher-order thinking skills to the newly acquired vocabulary.

The **Critical Thinking Activity** involves the student in the process of conceptualizing, applying, analyzing, synthesizing, and/or evaluating information related to the passage.

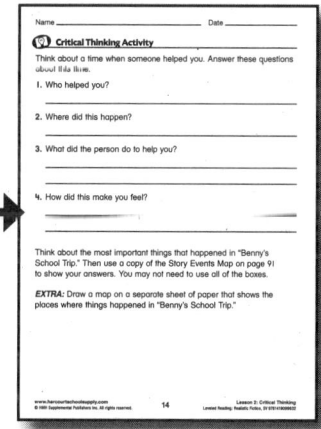

Page 4 features a helpful **Passage Titles and Levels Chart** for easy reference, and page 5 consists of a **Series Scope and Sequence Chart** that lists the page numbers where specific skills are utilized within the four-book series.

Pages 88–93 are graphic organizers. Some Critical Thinking Activity pages utilize these graphic organizers; however, the graphic organizers may also be utilized as pre- or post-reading activities to additionally support reading of the passages.

An answer key is found on pages 94–96.

Passage Titles and Levels Chart

Passage Title	Grade Level	F&P Level	DRA Level
Whistle Like a Bird	K–1	D	8
Benny's School Trip	1	G	14
I Can Be Anything	1	E	14
A Penny Changes the Day	1–2	H	18
Nana's Kitchen	1–2	H	18
The Around-the-World Lunch	1–2	I	20
The Missing Pet	2	K	24
A Gift to Share	2	K	24
My Prairie Summer	2–3	M	34
Milo's Great Invention	2–3	M	34
The School Mural	2–3	M	34
Diary of a Pioneer Boy	3–4	Q	40
The Grand Canyon Doesn't Scare Me	4–5	T	50

Levels in this chart are subjective. Educators are encouraged to freely adjust designated levels according to their personal evaluation.

Grade Level represents the grade level at which the text is written and the level at which the student is reading.

F&P Level = Fountas and Pinnell Guided Reading Level
Matching Books to Readers, Using Leveled Books in Guided Reading K–3.
Irene C. Fountas and Gay Su Pinnell. Heinemann, 1999.
Guiding Readers and Writers 3–6. Irene C. Fountas and Gay Su Pinnell.
Heinemann, 2001.

DRA Level = Developmental Reading Assessment Level
Developmental Reading Assessment Resource Guide.
Joetta Beaver, Celebration Press, 1997.

Series Scope and Sequence Chart

Reading Skills	Science	Social Studies	Realistic Fiction	Tales
COMPREHENSION				
Literal Comprehension				
Understanding Facts and Details	7, 11, 16, 21, 26, 31, 37, 39, 44, 52, 60, 69, 78, 80, 87	7, 11, 16, 21, 27, 34, 72, 80, 87	7, 12, 17, 22, 27, 32, 38, 44, 59, 68, 73, 82	22, 69
Identifying Plot			7, 22, 24, 34, 38, 44, 46, 59, 61, 73	7, 11, 16, 28, 30, 43, 45, 51, 69, 77, 86
Identifying Main Idea and Supporting Details	7, 11, 16, 21, 26, 31, 37, 44, 52, 60, 69, 78, 87	7, 11, 21, 27, 34, 41, 43, 47, 63, 72, 89	12, 27, 52	28, 60, 77
Summarizing	23, 27, 37, 61, 78, 80	47, 87	38, 82	30, 43
Interpretive Skills				
Retelling	9, 33, 39, 70, 79, 87	56	17, 24, 87	77
Distinguishing Fact from Opinion	7, 31, 54, 78	16, 87	59	
Sequencing	18, 69	34, 36, 49, 74	7, 12, 29, 34, 40, 44, 68, 73, 78, 87	7, 61, 77
Identifying Cause and Effect	37, 54, 60, 89	23, 41	12, 22, 52, 69, 73, 87	35, 51, 53, 69, 86, 88
Recognizing Setting			32, 46, 61	35, 45, 61, 86
Comparing and Contrasting	16, 33, 44, 62	9, 16, 21, 27, 47, 56, 63, 72	52, 54, 78	18, 22, 35, 43, 51, 77, 86
Interpreting Text Features		41, 63		11
Critical Thinking				
Categorizing and Classifying	21, 33	17, 87	38	
Creative Response	9, 13, 18, 23, 28, 89	9, 13, 18, 29, 36, 43, 49, 65, 74	9, 14, 19, 24, 40, 46, 54, 61, 69, 78, 87	9, 13, 37, 45, 53, 71
Understanding Realism and Fantasy	23, 46		32, 38, 73	11, 16, 22, 28, 51
Making Predictions	39		7, 27	11, 28
Drawing Conclusions	7, 11, 26, 28, 38, 52, 54, 69, 78, 79	16, 27, 47, 54, 63	22, 38, 52, 53, 68, 82	9, 13, 45, 53
Identifying Author's Purpose	7, 11, 16, 21, 28, 44, 54, 62, 69, 78	11, 21, 41, 80	12, 68, 82	16, 35, 43
Analyzing Character		54	7, 12, 22, 24, 27, 28, 38, 52, 54, 73, 78, 87	7, 11, 22, 28, 30, 35, 43, 51, 60, 62, 69, 77, 86, 88
Making Inferences	7, 13, 16, 21, 27, 31, 38, 60	7, 16, 21, 27, 41, 47, 54	27, 32, 44, 73	16, 28, 43, 51, 61, 69
Making Judgments	33, 39, 46, 70	23, 80, 89		13, 35
Identifying Theme			87	16, 22, 69, 79, 86
Identifying Genre		54, 80		16, 28, 35, 69
Application of Newly Acquired Knowledge	13, 18, 23, 32, 37, 44, 46, 54, 61, 62, 69, 71, 80, 87, 89	13, 23, 29, 36, 43, 49, 65, 74	9, 19, 34, 40, 69, 78	9, 24
VOCABULARY				
Naming Words				23, 70
Rhyming Words	32, 38, 70	28	8, 60	8, 17, 23
Classifying	37	17	23, 28, 45, 53	29
Context Clues	8, 12, 17, 22, 27, 31, 32, 38, 45, 53, 61, 70, 79	8, 12, 22, 28, 35, 48, 55, 64, 81, 88	8, 13, 23, 33, 39, 45, 53, 60, 67, 77, 86	8, 12, 17, 23, 29, 44, 52, 61, 70, 78, 87
Synonyms	22, 32, 38, 45, 53, 79, 88	35	13, 18, 28, 60, 77, 86	29, 70
Antonyms	17, 32, 70	12, 22, 28, 81	60, 86	8, 29, 70, 78
Words with Multiple Meanings		88	8, 18, 39	17, 23, 61, 70, 78
Prefixes			13	78
Suffixes			13, 86	17, 23, 44
Phonics	32, 70	12		
Compound Words		28, 81	13, 23, 33	61

www.harcourtschoolsupply.com
© HMH Supplemental Publishers Inc. All rights reserved.

Series Scope and Sequence Chart
Leveled Reading: Realistic Fiction, SV 9781419099632

Name _____   Date _____

Get Ready to Read

Have you ever made music? You may have sung a song or played a piano. Read about one child who makes music with her grandmother.

Whistle Like a Bird

I want to **whistle** like a bird.

Grandma shows me how to whistle like a bird.

I want to **howl** like a dog.

Grandma shows me how to howl like a dog.

I want to sing like a **star.**

Grandma shows me how to sing like a star.

Together we make a **concert.**

Name _____ Date _____

 Reading Comprehension Check

Circle the letter next to the **best** answer.

1. What does the writer want to learn to do first?
   A whistle like a bird
   B howl like a dog
   C sing like a star
   D play with Grandma

2. As a result of Grandma's lessons, what will the writer be able to do?
   A build a bird cage with Grandma
   B train dogs to scare away robbers
   C make a concert with Grandma
   D name the stars in the sky

3. According to the story, what kind of sound does a dog make?
   A It whistles.
   B It sings.
   C It barks.
   D It howls.

4. Based on the tone of the story, what is most likely to happen in future years between the writer and Grandma?
   A The writer will become bored with Grandma.
   B The writer will continue to spend time with Grandma.
   C The writer will move far away from Grandma.
   D The writer and Grandma will write a book about birds.

Answer the questions below in complete sentences.

5. What is this story mostly about?
   _____
   _____

6. What kind of relationship do you think the writer has with Grandma?
   _____
   _____

Name _____ Date _____

 Vocabulary Practice

Choose a word from the box to complete each sentence. Write each word on the line.

| together   star   howl   concert   whistle |

1. In this story, a _____ is a person many people know about because he or she does something well.

2. The word *growl* rhymes with _____.

3. If you _____, you make music with your lips.

4. The word _____ means "with one another."

5. At a _____, one or more persons sing or play music or do both.

 Vocabulary Extension

Use a vocabulary word in a fun way! Draw a picture to go with each sentence.

| Wolves **howl** when the moon is full. | Do you know how to **whistle?** |

Name _____ Date _____

 **Critical Thinking Activity**

1. Some things make sounds. Here are three examples:

   A cat meows.

   A bee buzzes.

   Thunder rumbles.

   Think of four other things that make sounds. Then complete the sentences below with those four things and sounds.

   I want to _____ like _____.

   I want to _____ like _____.

   I want to _____ like _____.

   I want to _____ like _____.

   You have made up a poem! Read your poem to someone. When you say each word that names a sound, try to make the word be like that sound.

2. Draw a picture in the box below to go with the poem you wrote.

Name _____ Date _____

Get Ready to Read

Think about a school trip you have taken. What was it like? Did you lose anything? In this story, a boy goes on a school trip to the zoo and has problems. Read "Benny's School Trip" to find out what his problems are.

Benny's School Trip

Benny was too happy to think!
Today his class was going to the zoo.

Benny went to school without his **lunchbox.**
Benny's dad took the lunchbox to him.

All the children got on the bus to go to the zoo.
Benny **forgot** his lunchbox again.
Benny's teacher took the lunchbox to him.

All the children got off the bus at the zoo.
Benny forgot his lunchbox again.
The bus **driver** took the lunchbox to him.

Name _____ Date _____

The children saw monkeys and other animals.
Then they stopped for lunch.

Benny **cried,** "Oh no, my lunch is missing!"
So everyone looked for Benny's lunch.

They went back to see the monkeys.
One monkey was eating a banana.
Benny **wondered** if that was his banana.

They went back to see the elephants.
One elephant was eating peanuts.
Benny wondered if those were his peanuts.

Then Benny **remembered** that he put his lunch in his backpack.
But Benny could not find his backpack.

Benny's teacher said, "Benny, your backpack is on your back!"
So Benny had lunch at the zoo after all.

Name _____ Date _____

✓ Reading Comprehension Check

Complete each sentence below. Use what you read in the story.

1. The setting of the story is _____.

2. Benny's first problem is _____
   _____.

3. The students see animals such as _____ and
   _____.

4. A good word to describe Benny is _____.

5. The final problem that Benny has is _____
   _____.

6. Benny's teacher, Benny's father, and the bus driver are alike when
   they _____.

7. Because Benny's teacher says, "Benny, your backpack is on your
   back!", Benny is able to _____
   _____.

8. The writer's purpose in writing this story is most likely to _____
   _____.

Name _____   Date _____

 Vocabulary Practice

Write the vocabulary word from the box that fits each clue to finish the puzzle.

| lunchbox | cried | driver |
| remembered | forgot | wondered |

Across
3. shouted
5. thought about again
6. compound word that names a thing in which you carry food

Down
1. wanted to know
2. someone who guides or controls a car
4. did not remember

Name _____   Date _____

 **Critical Thinking Activity**

Think about a time when someone helped you. Answer these questions about this time.

1. Who helped you?

   _____

2. Where did this happen?

   _____

3. What did the person do to help you?

   _____

   _____

4. How did this make you feel?

   _____

   _____

Think about the most important things that happened in "Benny's School Trip." Then use a copy of the Story Events Map on page 91 to show your answers. You may not need to use all of the boxes.

EXTRA: Draw a map on a separate sheet of paper that shows the places where things happened in "Benny's School Trip."

Name _____ Date _____

Get Ready to Read

What kind of jobs do you do at home and at school? How can doing these jobs help you when you grow up? You may already know what kind of job you would like to have when you grow up. The child in this story believes he can have any job in the future.

I Can Be Anything

When I grow up, I can be anything.

When I grow up, I can be a painter.
I will paint and sell beautiful paintings.

When I grow up, I can be a vet.
I will care for pets and farm animals.

When I grow up, I can be a dentist.
I will care for teeth and **gums.**

When I grow up, I can be a pianist.
I will play concerts all over the world.

When I grow up, I can be a singer.
I will sing songs and be a star.

Name _____ Date _____

When I grow up, I can be a race car driver.
I will win many races and have a large **fan** club.

When I grow up, I can be a tennis champ.
I will play hard and win every **match.**

When I grow up, I can be an acrobat.
I will turn and spin and be a circus star.

When I grow up, I can be a dancer.
I will tap-dance on a **wooden** stage.

When I grow up, I can be a teacher.
I will help children learn how to read.

When I grow up, I can be a writer.
I will write funny stories and make people laugh.

When I grow up, I can be a pilot.
I will fly a jet and take people places.

When I grow up, I can be an astronaut.
I will fly to Mars and other planets.

But for now, I will just be a kid!

Name _____ Date _____

✓ Reading Comprehension Check

Complete each sentence below.

1. A _____ makes sick dogs, horses, and cows well again.

2. Two things an acrobat does are _____ and _____.

3. A _____ takes people places in a jet.

4. A pianist plays _____ in many different places.

5. An _____ flies to other planets.

6. A tap-dancer dances on a _____.

7. A _____ takes care of people's teeth.

8. A writer makes people laugh with his or her funny _____.

Name _____   Date _____

 **Vocabulary Practice**

Circle the letter next to the **best** answer.

1. In this story, *gums* means—
   A things that make a loud noise.
   B parts of the inside of your mouth.
   C some things you chew that taste good.
   D places to play games indoors.

2. In this story, *wooden* means—
   A made of wood.
   B very big.
   C only for children.
   D make-believe.

3. In this story, *match* means—
   A a clock.
   B to make two things go together.
   C something for starting a fire.
   D a game.

4. In this story, *fan* means—
   A a thing that makes people feel cool.
   B to blow air on someone.
   C to have a good time.
   D a person who likes something a lot.

 **Vocabulary Extension**

Choose your favorite vocabulary word. Write it in the chart below. Then write what the word means in your own words. Draw a picture to illustrate the word and help you remember it in the future.

Word:	
Definition in my own words:	
Illustration:	

Name _____ Date _____

💡 Critical Thinking Activity

Think of three things you can be when you grow up. Think about why you would you like to be these things. Then complete the sentences.

1. When I grow up, I can be _____

   _____.

   I would like to be this because _____

   _____

   _____.

2. When I grow up, I can be _____

   _____.

   I would like to be this because _____

   _____

   _____.

3. When I grow up, I can be _____

   _____.

   I would like to be this because _____

   _____

   _____.

EXTRA: Find pictures in books or magazines of people doing different jobs. Cut out the pictures and glue them on a poster.

Name _____ Date _____

Get Ready to Read

Have you ever heard the saying, "See a penny. Pick it up. All that day you'll have good luck!"? Think about how a penny can change someone's life. Read about a girl who finds a lucky penny on her shopping trip.

A Penny Changes the Day

Grandpa saw Nikki's **frown.** "Why do you look so sad?" he asked.

"I'm not having a very good day," answered Nikki.

"Why don't you go shopping with me?" asked Grandpa. "Maybe we can turn that frown upside down!"

Grandpa pointed to something **shiny.** "See a penny," he said. "Pick it up. All that day you'll have good luck!"

"A penny can't change my day," said Nikki.

"A penny *can* change your day," said Grandpa.

Nikki picked up the penny.

"Your day is getting better already," he said. "You have one cent more than you had this morning."

They went to buy some nails for Grandpa. Nikki saw something silver in the **bin** of nails.

"Look! I found a **nickel!**" Nikki said. "A nickel is worth 5 pennies."

"Now you have 6 cents altogether!" said Grandpa.

Name _____   Date _____

Next they went to buy a book for Grandpa. Nikki's penny fell onto the floor. She looked under every **bookshelf.** Nikki said, "Look! Here's my penny and a **dime,** too! A dime is worth 10 pennies."

"Now you have 16 cents altogether!" said Grandpa.

Then they went to buy some shoes for Grandpa. Nikki saw a big **coin** in her chair. She shouted, "I found a **quarter!** It is worth 25 pennies."

"Now you have 41 cents altogether!" said Grandpa.

"Grandpa, you were right," said Nikki. "The penny has brought me good luck!"

"It made you smile, too," added Grandpa. "Now it's time to go home."

"May we go to one more store?" asked Nikki.

Nikki and Grandpa went inside the bakery. Grandpa helped Nikki count her money. "I can buy each of us a cookie," said Nikki. "And I get to keep my lucky penny, too!"

Name _____ Date _____

✓ Reading Comprehension Check

Answer each question in complete sentences.

1. Why is Nikki frowning at the beginning of the story?

   _____

   _____

2. How much money does Nikki find altogether?

   _____

3. What kind of person do you think Grandpa is? Give an example from the story to show this.

   _____

   _____

   _____

4. What is the last stop Nikki and Grandpa make before they go home?

   _____

5. If Nikki's luck continues at the bakery, what will most likely happen there?

   _____

   _____

6. What happens as a result of Nikki finding the penny?

   _____

   _____

Name _____ Date _____

 ## Vocabulary Practice

Write the words from the box to complete the paragraphs.

shiny	bookshelf	dime
quarter	coin	bin
frown	nickel	

Jane liked to save money in her piggy bank. She kept the piggy bank next to the books on her (**1.**) _____.

One day she took down the piggy bank to count her money. "Oh, no!" Jane shouted with a (**2.**) _____ on her face. "I have only one (**3.**) _____, which is 5 cents. And I have only one (**4.**) _____, which is 10 cents. Altogether I have 15 cents. That is not very much!"

Jane looked in the (**5.**) _____ where she kept all her toys. She saw something (**6.**) _____ inside. It was a (**7.**) _____. Jane said, "Now I have 25 cents more. That makes 40 cents altogether." Then she saw a brown (**8.**) _____ on the floor. She said, "With this penny, I have 41 cents."

Jane was happier. She had 26 cents more than she did before.

www.harcourtschoolsupply.com
© HMH Supplemental Publishers Inc. All rights reserved.

Lesson 4: Vocabulary
Leveled Reading: Realistic Fiction, SV 9781419099632

Name _____ Date _____

💡 Critical Thinking Activity

1. Imagine that you are Nikki and it is the day after you went shopping with Grandpa. Write a letter to a friend. Tell your friend about all the things that happened to you when you were with Grandpa.

Dear _____,

_____

_____

_____

_____

_____

_____

_____

_____

_____

_____

_____

_____

_____

2. Think about how Nikki changes in the story. Use a copy of the Character Change Story Map on page 89 to show your answer.

Name _____ Date _____

Get Ready to Read

Who has helped you cook something for yourself or your family? What did you do first? The boy in this story loves cooking with his grandmother. Read about something she gives him so he can make the special dish with his mom.

Nana's Kitchen

"Nana, I'm here!" called John Claude. He ran into his grandmother's kitchen. "It smells good in here," John Claude told Nana. "It makes me hungry. Can we have egg nests?" he asked. "Mom doesn't know how to make them."

Nana nodded. "I will be the cook," Nana said. "You can be the helper," she told him. Nana got a **spatula** and her **special** black pan.

John Claude got out eggs and bread. Then he **gathered** a small glass, a cup, and a fork. He used the glass to cut holes in the bread.

"I want to crack an egg," John Claude said. He hit an egg on the cup. Egg **splattered** all over. "Uh-oh," he said and looked at Nana.

Nana smiled and cleaned up the mess. "Watch me," she told John Claude.

Nana tapped an egg on the **rim** of the cup. John Claude **gently** tapped an egg, too. It cracked just right. Then Nana showed him how to open his egg. It slid into the cup. "I did it!" John Claude said with a grin.

Name _____ Date _____

Nana put the bread in the pan and let it brown. Then she turned the bread over.

"What do I do now?" John Claude asked.

"You beat the eggs," Nana said.

John Claude got the fork. He beat the eggs until Nana said to stop.

Nana **poured** the eggs into the bread holes. John Claude listened to the eggs **sizzle.**

"I like cooking with you," he told Nana. "And I like egg nests a lot," he added.

"You're a good helper," Nana told John Claude. "My special pan helps, too," she added.

Nana put the egg nests on plates. John Claude took a bite of his egg nest. "I wish my mom had a special pan," he said. "Then she could make egg nests."

Nana looked out at her backyard. John Claude could tell she was thinking.

"I want you to have my special pan," Nana said. "You can teach your mom to make egg nests."

"Will you come eat with us?" asked John Claude. "You can be the helper, and I will be the cook!"

Name _____ Date _____

 Reading Comprehension Check

Circle the letter next to the **best** answer.

1. After John Claude cracks an egg the first time, he thinks—
   A that he will not get to eat.
   B that he will have to go home.
   C that Nana will get mad.
   D that he did a good job.

2. Nana shows John Claude how to—
   A beat an egg.
   B cut holes in bread.
   C put the bread in a pan.
   D crack an egg.

3. What does Nana have that is special for cooking egg nests?
   A a pan
   B a spatula
   C a cup
   D a fork

4. What will probably happen the next time Nana visits John Claude?
   A His mom will make egg nests.
   B He will make egg nests.
   C He will not crack an egg right.
   D He will be Nana's helper.

Answer the questions below in complete sentences.

5. What does John Claude do that makes him feel proud?

_____

_____

6. What is this story mostly about?

_____

_____

www.harcourtschoolsupply.com
© HMH Supplemental Publishers Inc. All rights reserved.

27

Lesson 5: Reading Comprehension
Leveled Reading: Realistic Fiction, SV 9781419099632

Name _____ Date _____

 Vocabulary Practice

Choose a word from the box that best fits with each group of words. Write the word on the line.

| sizzle | poured | spatula |

1. pan, fork, _____

2. buzz, pop, hiss, _____

3. stirred, beat, _____

Choose a word from the box that can take the place of the underlined word or words in the sentence. Write the word on the line.

| special | rim | splattered | gathered | gently |

4. Kyle's tooth hit the underline{edge} of the glass. _____

5. The teacher underline{put together} the children's artwork. _____

6. "This plate is underline{different}," said Mr. Lee. _____

7. The can of paint fell, and paint underline{splashed} on Eva. _____

8. Paul underline{softly} tapped his fingers on his desk. _____

 **Vocabulary Extension**

Write a word in each box that will help you remember what the word in each oval means.

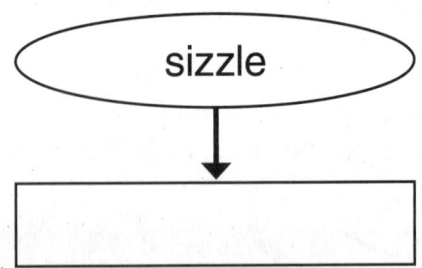
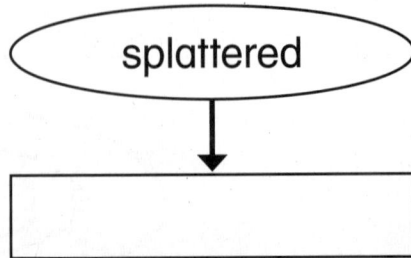

28

www.harcourtschoolsupply.com
© HMH Supplemental Publishers Inc. All rights reserved.

Lesson 5: Vocabulary
Leveled Reading: Realistic Fiction, SV 9781419099632

Name _____ Date _____

 **Critical Thinking Activity**

1. What are the steps that Nana and John Claude follow to make egg nests? Write the steps in the boxes below. The first step has been done for you.

   1. _Gather a spatula, special pan, glass, fork, cup, bread, and eggs._

   2. _____

   3. _____

   4. _____

   5. _____

   6. _____

2. What is John Claude like? What does he like to do? Complete a copy of the Character Traits Web on page 90 to tell about John Claude.

Name _____   Date _____

Get Ready to Read

Do you or your friends bring a lunch from home to eat at school? Think of the foods from different parts of the world that might be in a lunch. In this story, Pepito's aunt packs a special lunch just for him. He wonders what the food will taste like.

The Around-the-World Lunch

Pepito's aunt was in town for a visit. She had packed his lunch for school. She said, "I put a surprise food from Cuba in your lunch. It's a Cuban **sandwich.** Don't look inside the bag until **lunchtime.**"

Pepito was so excited. He loved sandwiches. He loved surprises. He wondered what a Cuban sandwich was like. Pepito could hardly wait until lunchtime.

At school Pepito told his friends about the surprise food. He said, "My aunt made me a Cuban sandwich. But I don't know how it **tastes.**"

"Maybe it tastes like peanut butter and jelly," said Lee. "Or maybe it tastes like pizza."

"My grandfather cooks lunch for me," said Lee. "He makes foods from China. I like it when he makes won tons. Won tons are like stuffed dumplings."

Name _____ Date _____

"My aunt cooks plantains to go with my lunch," said Tara. "It's a food from Africa. A plantain tastes like a fried banana. It's sweet and **mushy.**"

"My dad cooks poori to go with my lunch," said Ray. "He cooks food from India all the time. He taught me how to cook poori. Poori is fried bread."

"My mom cooks buñuelos to go with my lunch," said Ana. "Buñuelos are a food from Mexico. They taste like flat, **crunchy** doughnuts. I love to eat buñuelos."

At noon the bell rang, and everyone went to lunch. Pepito pulled out the Cuban sandwich. He took one big bite. Pepito said, "Mmmm, I know what this tastes like. It tastes like a ham and cheese sandwich!"

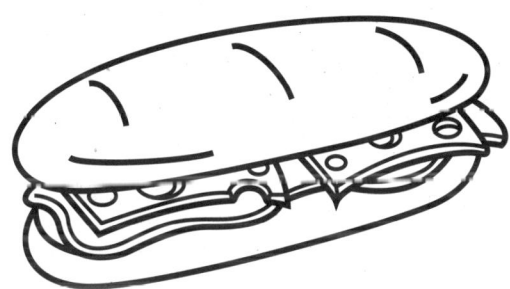

Name _____   Date _____

 **Reading Comprehension Check**
_____

Circle the letter next to the **best** answer.

1. Pepito's aunt—
   A hates to cook Cuban food for Pepito.
   B talks to Pepito's class about Cuban food.
   C makes a Cuban sandwich for Pepito's lunch.
   D travels to Cuba to make sandwiches for children.

2. This story does NOT include a food from—
   A China.
   B Greece.
   C India.
   D Cuba.

3. This story takes place mostly at—
   A Pepito's home.
   B Lee's home.
   C Pepito's school.
   D Ana's home.

4. The author most likely wrote this passage to—
   A persuade readers to begin eating healthy foods.
   B entertain readers with a story about caring families.
   C inform readers about the importance of a well-balanced diet.
   D help readers appreciate foods from other countries.

Answer the questions below in complete sentences.

5. Does Pepito like the sandwich when he finally eats it? What clue from the story tells you he feels this way?

_____

_____

6. What are two events from the story that can happen in real life?

_____

_____

Name _____ Date _____

 Vocabulary Practice

Choose a word from the box to complete each sentence. Write each word on the line.

| tastes   crunchy   sandwich   lunchtime |

1. Popcorn is fun to eat because it is _____.

2. The word _____ is a compound word made from two smaller words.

3. A _____ is made with bread and other food items.

4. Food _____ really good when you are hungry.

 **Vocabulary Extension**

Write a clue in the triangle for the word in the oval. Then write a sentence in the rectangle that uses the word.

crunchy

Name _____   Date _____

💡 Critical Thinking Activity

1. Use a copy of the Story Events Map on page 91 to tell what happens in the story. You may not need to use all of the boxes.

2. Complete the chart below using what you learned in the story.

What is the food?	Where is it from?	What is it like?
won tons	China	like stuffed dumplings
plaintains		
poori		
buñuelos		
Cuban sandwich		

3. Imagine you are Pepito. Write a thank-you note to your aunt to thank her for making you a Cuban sandwich.

_____
_____
_____
_____
_____
_____

EXTRA: Find out about two more foods from other countries. Find out what they are like. Add this information to the chart above.

Name _____ Date _____

Get Ready to Read

Suppose you have a missing pet. What do you do? Where do you look for it? Read on to find out where people in a neighborhood go looking for a missing pet.

The Missing Pet

James was in a hurry to get home. He wanted to play with his pet parrot Oliver. James opened the door and ran up to his room. He looked in the cage, but Oliver wasn't there.

"Mom, have you seen Oliver?" called James. "He's not in his cage."

"No, but I'll help you look for him," Mom said. She saw a **clue** and pointed to the window. She said, "Look! The window is open. Maybe he flew outside."

James and Mom went outside. They saw Cassie playing. "Have you seen my parrot?" James asked. "He's missing."

"No, but I'll help you look for him," Cassie said. She saw a clue and pointed to the sidewalk. "Look! There's a yellow feather. Maybe he flew this way."

James, Mom, and Cassie ran down the sidewalk. They saw Chris on a bike. "Have you seen my parrot?" James asked.

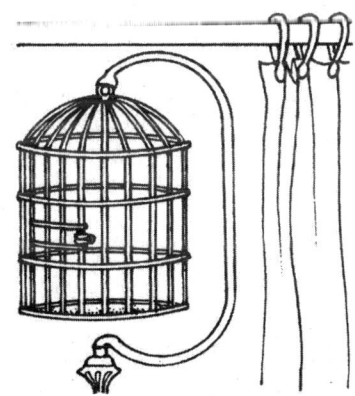

"No, but I'll help you look for him," Chris said. He saw a clue and pointed to the bushes. "Look! There's a red feather. Maybe he flew this way."

James, Mom, Cassie, and Chris ran farther down the sidewalk. They saw Ana roller-skating. "Have you seen my parrot?" James asked.

"No, but I'll help you look for him," Ana said. She saw a clue and pointed to the grass. "Look! There's an orange feather. Maybe he flew this way."

James, Mom, Cassie, Chris, and Ana ran farther down the sidewalk. They saw Mrs. Chang planting flowers. "Have you seen my parrot?" James asked.

"No, but I'll help you look for him," Mrs. Chang said. She saw a clue and pointed to the garden. "Look! There's a green feather. Maybe he flew this way."

James, Mom, Cassie, Chris, Ana, and Mrs. Chang ran farther down the sidewalk. They saw Mr. Ford painting. "Have you seen my parrot?" James asked.

"No, I haven't, but I'll help you look for him," Mr. Ford said. He saw a clue and pointed to the grass. "Look! There's a purple feather. Maybe he flew this way."

James, Mom, Cassie, Chris, Ana, Mrs. Chang, and Mr. Ford ran farther down the sidewalk. As they got near the park, James stopped. He said, "Wait! Oliver doesn't have purple feathers!"

"No? Well, let's look anyway," said Mr. Ford. "There are many birds at the park. Maybe Oliver is there."

Name _____ Date _____

James, Mom, Cassie, Chris, Ana, Mrs. Chang, and Mr. Ford ran to the park. James said, "There are birds everywhere! How will I find Oliver?"

"Maybe Oliver will find you," said Mr. Ford.

James called out, "Oliver! Where are you?" Suddenly Oliver flew down and **landed** on James's **shoulder.** Then a yellow, red, orange, green, and PURPLE parrot flew down. It landed on James's other shoulder.

Mr. Ford said, "James, it looks like Oliver found a friend. I guess you'll have to keep them both."

James looked at Mom and said, "May I please keep Oliver's new friend?"

Mom said, "First let's find out if someone is missing him. We need to **post** signs in the neighborhood. If no one **claims** him, you may keep him."

James, Mom, Cassie, Chris, Ana, Mrs. Chang, and Mr. Ford walked home. Oliver and his new friend flew home with them. As the parrots flew, they did flips, dips, dives, and **twirls.**

Mr. Ford, Mrs. Chang, Ana, Chris, and Cassie stopped at their houses and said, "Goodbye. Take care of Oliver and his new friend."

James said, "I will. Thanks for helping me." James and Mom waved goodbye and went home.

When they got home, Mom asked, "What will you name Oliver's new friend?"

James said, "I know! I'll call him Lucky. He's lucky to have a home, and Oliver is lucky to have a new friend."

Name _____ Date _____

✓ Reading Comprehension Check

Circle the letter next to the **best** answer.

1. Which of these helps you the MOST to know that James really likes Oliver?
   A He wants to call Oliver's new friend Lucky.
   B At the park he says there are birds everywhere.
   C He asks his mom if he can keep Oliver's new friend.
   D He hurries home to play with Oliver.

2. Which clue is NOT a clue for finding Oliver?
   A an open window
   B a red feather
   C a purple feather
   D an orange feather

3. What do Cassie, Chris, Ana, Mrs. Chang, and Mr. Ford have in common?
   A They like Oliver as much as James does.
   B They want to help James.
   C They are playing outside.
   D They have seen Oliver.

4. What does James have to do before he can keep the other parrot?
   A find out if someone is missing the parrot
   B give the parrot a name
   C see if the parrot likes its new home
   D show that he can take care of two parrots

Answer the questions below in complete sentences.

5. Is anything in this story make-believe—something that could not happen in real life? If something is make-believe, tell what it is.

   _____

   _____

6. In your own words, tell what this story is about.

   _____

   _____

Name _____ Date _____

Vocabulary Practice

Read each sentence. Circle the letter next to the **best** meaning for the underlined word.

1. The bee landed on the flower.
   A buzzed loudly
   B came down after flying
   C moved around in a circle
   D ate something

2. The glove on the ground was a clue about where the man was.
   A something that helps to solve a mystery
   B something that is heard the first time
   C a thing that has been lost
   D a thing used to play a game

3. The teacher will post the list of students who are in the play.
   A a tall piece of wood
   B things sent in the mail
   C put up
   D call about

4. Mom's bag was on her shoulder.
   A hook on a door
   B small table next to a bed
   C part of a person's legs
   D part of the body near an arm

5. If Danny claims the kitten, he can take it home.
   A wants to take care of something
   B says that something is his
   C starts to like something a lot
   D feels happy about something

6. The little girl did five twirls one right after the other.
   A dances
   B kicks
   C spins
   D jumps

Vocabulary Extension

Write a word in each box that will help you remember what the word in each oval means.

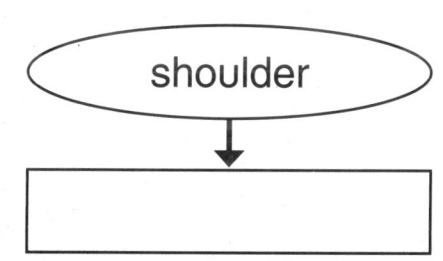

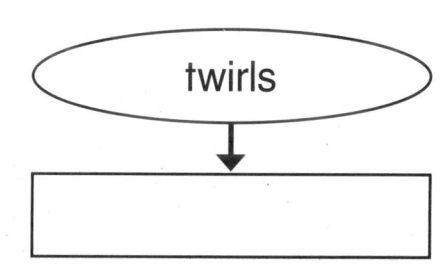

(shoulder)   (twirls)

Name _____ Date _____

💡 Critical Thinking Activity

1. Write a story about a boy or girl who solved a problem with the help of one or more persons. Make the problem different from the problem that James had. On the lines below, write a story about how the boy or girl solved the problem. (If you run out of space, you may finish your story on another sheet of paper.)

   Before you start writing your story, think about these things:
   - When and where will the story happen?
   - What is the problem?
   - What do people do to help the boy or girl solve the problem?
   - How does the boy or girl feel after the problem is solved?

   _____
   _____
   _____
   _____
   _____
   _____
   _____
   _____
   _____
   _____

2. Draw a map of James's neighborhood. Show the places where things happened in "The Missing Pet." Write the names of the places on your map. Write numbers on your map that show the correct order of the places where things happened in the story.

Name _____ Date _____

Get Ready to Read

Think about the best gift you have ever received or given. Describe the gift. Was it bought at a store? Was it made by you or someone else? In this story, Mattie wants to give a birthday gift. Each thing she wants to give either costs too much or is just not right. Will Mattie find a gift that is just right?

A Gift to Share

Soon it would be Aunt Debra's birthday. Everyone in Mattie's family had a present for her **except** Mattie. She thought all week about what to give Aunt Debra. She wanted to give her the best gift ever.

Mattie knew Aunt Debra would love a new book. Mattie shook her piggy bank. She had only $1.78. That would not be enough to buy a new book. Mattie thought hard. What could she get Aunt Debra?

Mattie saw her brother and asked, "What do you think would be the best gift ever?"

He said, "A football, of course."

Mattie said, "Thanks, but I don't think that's the best gift ever." She knew Aunt Debra wouldn't want a football. Mattie thought hard. What could she get her?

Name _____ Date _____

Next Mattie saw her **cousin.** Mattie asked, "What do you think would be the best gift ever?"

He said, "A car, of course."

Mattie said, "Thanks, but that's not the best gift ever." She knew she couldn't buy her a car. Mattie thought hard. What could she get her?

Mattie ran to the store and found Aunt Debra's **favorite magazine.** Mattie hoped she would have enough money. But it cost too much. Mattie thought hard. What could she get Aunt Debra?

Mattie asked Mom, "What do you think would be the best gift ever?"

Mom said, "Well, sometimes the best gifts come from the heart. Could you make something yourself to share with Aunt Debra?"

Mattie thought hard. What could she make? She could make a vase, but she didn't have any **clay.** She could paint a picture, but she didn't have any paint. She went outside to take a walk and think some more.

She walked toward Aunt Debra's house. She saw the **mail carrier** handing two boxes to her aunt. Aunt Debra said, "Great! They're here. I've been waiting for my new books. I just love to read."

Name _____ Date _____

    Mattie watched Aunt Debra open the boxes. Her aunt held the books with special care. Mattie smiled. This gave her a great idea. She thought, "I can make a book about me for Aunt Debra to read." She turned and ran home. She just knew that would be the best gift ever.

    Mattie ran upstairs to her favorite room. She got out her favorite book to see how it was made. Then she got out her art **supplies** and box of **photos**. Mattie picked out her brightest crayons and her best paper. She also picked out some special photos.

    Mattie folded the papers. She wrote a **title** on the first page. She glued photos on the next pages. She printed words in her best writing. She glued her favorite photo to the front for the cover. Then she wrapped the book in pretty paper.

    The next day Mattie gave Aunt Debra her gift. When Aunt Debra opened it, a big smile filled her face. She said, "This book is so special! It's better than any book I could ever buy." They looked at each photo of Mattie.

    Then Mattie had an idea. She found a photo of herself and Aunt Debra sitting together. She glued it on the last page. Aunt Debra looked at the photo and said, "Now the book is about us, too. This is the best gift ever."

Name _____ Date _____

✓ Reading Comprehension Check

Circle the letter next to the **best** answer.

1. Who is having a birthday?
   A Mattie
   B Aunt Debra
   C Mattie's cousin
   D Mattie' friend

2. What is Mattie's problem?
   A not enough money
   B too much money
   C not enough ideas
   D too many aunts

3. What is the second present idea given to Mattie?
   A a football
   B a magazine
   C a picture
   D a car

4. What happens that helps Mattie decide what to do for a present?
   A Mattie's brother tells her to buy a football.
   B Mattie's cousin shows her a new car.
   C The mail carrier hands Aunt Debra two boxes.
   D Mattie's mom gives her some money.

5. What does Mattie give Aunt Debra?
   A a magazine   C a vase
   B a book   D a picture

6. According to the story, what makes the best gift?
   A something you can read
   B something that costs a lot
   C something wrapped in paper
   D something from the heart

Answer the question below in complete sentences.

7. Do you think Aunt Debra is a special person to Mattie? Explain your answer. _____

_____

_____

Name _____ Date _____

✏️ Vocabulary Practice

Choose a word or words from the box that best fit with each group of words. Write the word on the line.

| cousin | supplies | mail carrier | magazine |

1. newspaper, book, _____
2. uncle, aunt, _____
3. paints, pencils, paper, _____
4. postcards, letters, _____

Choose a word from the box to complete each sentence. Write each word on the line.

| except | clay | photos | title | favorite |

5. The _____ of the book is *All About Me.*
6. Sanjay took lots of _____ of his friends.
7. The students made pots from _____.
8. Carlos finished all of his homework _____ math.
9. Lisa's _____ color is green.

✏️ Vocabulary Extension

Use a vocabulary word in a fun way! Draw a picture to go with each sentence.

Look at my **photos**!	My **cousin** is also my friend.

Name _____ Date _____

💡 Critical Thinking Activity

1. In the story, Mattie made Aunt Debra a gift "from the heart." For whom would you like to make a gift from the heart? What gift could you make for that person? How would you make the gift? Complete the sentences below.

    I would like to make a gift from the heart for _____
    _____.

    The gift I could make is _____
    _____.

    I would make the gift in the following way. _____
    _____
    _____
    _____
    _____
    _____
    _____
    _____

2. What is the story's setting? (*Setting* means where and when the story takes place.) Who are the characters? What is Mattie's problem? What is her solution? (*Solution* means how a problem is solved.) Use a copy of the Cluster Story Map on page 93 to answer these questions.

Name _____ Date _____

Get Ready to Read

What kinds of things are you afraid of? Are you afraid of the dark? Are you afraid of dogs? Read on to learn how Emma gets over her fear on the Oklahoma prairie.

My Prairie Summer

Going to Get Lucy

June 6, Morning

Dear **Diary,**

　We are on the way to pick up Lucy today! Mom, Dad, Ty, and I left the farm this morning. I sat in the back seat and watched the trailer wag behind our truck.

　On the way, Ty spotted a jackrabbit. Dad saw a hawk. Mom saw some purple coneflowers and pulled off the road. Everybody got out but me. I'm still sitting in the truck writing. Mom must be taking a **million** pictures! I sure wish they would hurry up. Lucy is waiting!

　FINALLY! I thought they'd never get back in the truck. Now we're going again. We just drove through a town. Mom always acts like she knows everybody. She was even waving at **strangers.** I **ducked** my head so they wouldn't see me.

Name _____ Date _____

Ty made me so mad when we drove past the town pool. Mom asked me if I was going to take swimming lessons this summer. Before I could even answer, Ty yelled that I wasn't because I was AFRAID! I'm not afraid. Well, maybe I'm a little scared of water.

June 6, Afternoon
Dear Diary,

Well, we made it to Leon Biggelo's ranch. I was so excited that I jumped right out of the truck and ran up to the porch. Leon came out laughing because I was in such a hurry. He took us out back to see Lucy. She is so beautiful! She is as tall as me and has brown hair and brown eyes. But she already weighs four hundred pounds! Lucy is our new buffalo! We will **protect** her on our ranch. She can run free on the plains.

I laughed when I saw Leon's sign: BIGGELO BUFFALO RANCH!

I asked Leon when Lucy was born. He said her birthday was in May. Me, too! Now we can **celebrate** our birthdays together. Leon showed me how to hold out long stems of grass so Lucy could eat them. She wrapped her **tongue** around them and ate them all! I wanted to get going so Lucy could meet our other buffaloes. But we had to stay and talk with Leon awhile. Dad and Leon led Lucy into the trailer. She was finally mine! Well, I mean OURS.

Ty and Mom went swimming at the pond when we got home. Not me. I stayed with Dad and helped feed Lucy. I hope she likes it here.

Name _____ Date _____

The Big Storm

July 11, Morning

Dear Diary,

　　Something was wrong with Lucy this morning. I held out a blade of bluestem grass, but she wouldn't eat it. Dad said Lucy was fine. He said that Lucy was just too hot to eat. Boy, it IS hot today!

　　Dad said going swimming would cool me off. I know what that means. It's time for my swimming lesson. I'd rather pick grasshoppers off the corn plants than swim. I am a little scared of the water, but I don't want Ty to know. Ty swims like a fish. He sort of looks like one, too. HA, HA!

July 11, Afternoon

Dear Diary,

　　I ALMOST floated today! Well, when Dad let go of me, I started to sink. I think I drank the whole pond. I came up **coughing.** Dad said maybe that was enough for one day. We got out of the water. Ty made his usual "quack, quack" noise, but none of the ducks quacked back. Now that was strange! The ducks always quacked with Ty. Today they seemed afraid of something.

Name _____ Date _____

   Suddenly it got dark, so I looked up. A huge black cloud was moving across the sky. It was like a giant mountain, all tall and wide.

   Dad told us to throw on our clothes and get going fast. I could tell he thought this would be a bad storm. We ran home. Just before we got home, the clouds got darker and darker. The wind blew dust in our faces. It started raining on us. We raced to the storm cellar. Mom was already there. She grabbed us all up in a tight hug and kissed us. I was scared. Ty was scared now, too.

   The rain and hail pounded against the storm cellar door. I didn't think it would ever stop. Mom sang songs with us, but I think she was scared, too. Dad kept checking the latch on the door. Finally it was quiet outside. Dad slowly opened the door. Everything seemed to be OK. Some **shutters** had come off our house. The animals in the barn were a little scared, but they were all right. Best of all, Lucy was OK!

Lucy Runs Away

August 2

Dear Diary,

   Lucy ran away today! Ty opened the gate, and she pushed right past him. It wasn't Ty's fault, but he was **upset.** I was out riding my horse, Daisy, so I went after Lucy. Ty, Mom, and Dad jumped in the truck and went after her, too. Lucy ran into the cornfield. The corn is taller than Dad now, so we couldn't see Lucy. Dad thought that maybe she would stop to eat because the corn is so sweet now. We all hoped she would.

Name _____ Date _____

I was scared for Lucy. Dad, Mom, and Ty drove around to one side of the field. I rode around to the other side. Lucy heard us and ran out of the field. Everyone else chased after her. I jumped off Daisy and stayed in the field in case Lucy turned around and came back. The tall grass brushed against me. The tiny bobwhites flew out of the grass. Lucy was heading for the pond. Now I was really scared. Lucy didn't know how to swim. Then I heard a loud splash!

I found Daisy and rode to the pond as fast as I could. I was sure something bad had happened to Lucy. By the time I got there, everybody was in the water. I slid off Daisy and ran to the pond. Lucy was swimming! I couldn't believe it. There she was swimming with Mom, Dad, and Ty. I just jumped in and started swimming with all of them.

Now both Lucy and I can swim! I'm sure glad Lucy is OK.

August 15
Dear Diary,

Today is really dry and dusty. It's a good thing I learned to swim this summer. That's the best way to cool off on a hot **prairie** day. Lucy even went to the pond with Ty and me this afternoon. Ty showed me how to swim underwater. Maybe he isn't such a bad brother after all.

School starts next week, so I'll only see Lucy after school. Maybe we'll have some adventures together this fall. When we do, I'll be sure to write it all down here.

EMMA

Name _____ Date _____

✓ Reading Comprehension Check

Answer each question in complete sentences.

1. In the first two paragraphs of the story, how does Emma feel? Tell why.

   _____

   _____

2. What is Emma's writing for "June 6, Afternoon" mostly about?

   _____

   _____

3. Why does Emma compare the storm cloud to a mountain?

   _____

   _____

4. Why is Emma "really scared" after Lucy has run away?

   _____

   _____

5. What makes Emma jump in the pond and start swimming?

   _____

   _____

6. What makes Emma start to think in a different way about her brother?

   _____

   _____

Name _____   Date _____

✏️ Vocabulary Practice

Choose a word from the box to complete each sentence. Write each word on the line.

diary	strangers	shutters
coughing	protect	ducked

1. No one knew the three _____ who had come to town.

2. The fence will _____ the chickens from foxes.

3. The tall man _____ so he would not hit his head on the tree branch.

4. Ross wrote in his _____ about his birthday party.

5. The wind made the _____ knock against the house.

6. Lisa has a sore throat and is _____ a lot.

Choose a word from the box that best fits with each group of words. Write the word on the line.

prairie	upset	tongue
million	celebrate	

7. hundred, thousand, _____

8. mouth, teeth, _____

9. angry, sad, _____

10. plains, fields, _____

11. birthday, party, _____

www.harcourtschoolsupply.com   53   Lesson 9: Vocabulary
© HMH Supplemental Publishers Inc. All rights reserved.   Leveled Reading: Realistic Fiction, SV 9781419099632

Name _____ Date _____

💡 Critical Thinking Activity

1. How are Emma and Ty alike and different? Use a copy of the the Compare and Contrast Chart on page 92 to show your answers.

2. Imagine that you can have an unusual animal for a pet. What pet would you have? Think what it would be like to have this pet. On the lines below, write two times in a diary about having this pet.

DATE: _____

_____
_____
_____
_____
_____

DATE: _____

_____
_____
_____
_____
_____

EXTRA: In "My Prairie Summer," you learned a few facts about buffaloes. Find out three more facts about these animals. Look for facts in books or on the Internet.

Name _____   Date _____

Get Ready to Read

Think of a problem you have. Now imagine making a machine that would get rid of this problem. For example, suppose you have trouble waking up and getting ready for school. You might make a machine that gets you ready without waking you. In this story, Milo has a problem. He invents a machine to help him, but will it really work? Read on to see if Milo solves his problem.

Milo's Great Invention

Milo's mom and dad loved peas. Milo's big brother Ed loved peas. Milo's sister Anne loved peas. Well, their dog Snap didn't love peas. Milo did NOT love peas.

Milo tried to eat peas with butter and salt. He tried to eat peas with grape jelly. No matter what he tried, Milo still did not love peas. He didn't even like them. He needed to find a way to get rid of peas.

That night, Milo thought about his problem. He thought about how the peas would not go away. He had tried so many ways to get rid of peas, but nothing worked. He even put the peas in his shirt pocket, but his mom had found peas in the washing machine. He had a new idea. He would invent a machine to get rid of peas. Then he would never have to eat peas again! Milo decided he would start on his plan tomorrow.

Milo came home from school. He decided that he needed to learn more about peas. He put some **frozen** peas on his desk. Milo wrote down facts about peas.

Name _____   Date _____

Peas are green. Peas roll around. Round things can roll. "Aha!" Milo said to himself. "Peas can roll. That's it. I'll make peas roll in my **invention**!"

He tried rolling the peas down his shirt. He thought they would land in a bucket under his desk. But they got stuck on his clothes. He needed a better idea.

That night, Milo's family had peas for dinner again. Milo couldn't get the peas off his plate. He sat between his dad and Anne. If Anne saw him do something, she would tell on him. He couldn't feed them to his dog Snap because Snap wouldn't eat peas. He could cut a hole in the table, but that wouldn't be a very good idea. Milo knew he had to think of a way to get rid of peas.

Milo needed some ideas to build his invention. He looked around the house. First Milo found an old spoon in the kitchen. He also found a big roll of silver tape. In the **basement,** he found a long, thin **hose.** Peas could fit inside the hose.

In the garage, Milo saw a big vacuum cleaner. He looked at the long hose he had found. Then he looked at the big vacuum cleaner again. Milo got an idea.

Milo would **create** the Milo's Peas-Be-Gone machine. The machine would have three parts. The first part would be the special spoon with a hole in it. The second part would be a hose that hooked onto the spoon. The third part would be the big vacuum cleaner. The vacuum cleaner would hook onto the hose, making it a great invention! Milo sketched a drawing of his new idea. He labeled all three parts.

Name _____ Date _____

Milo needed help to build his great invention. He had to keep it a secret though. Milo asked Ed for help. "Can you make a hole in this spoon?" asked Milo.

"Sure, but why do you want a hole in it?" asked Ed. Then he frowned at Milo.

"Well, I'm going to make something **disappear**," said Milo, "but I need to keep it a secret."

Ed agreed to help Milo. Ed made a hole in the spoon. Milo was excited at the idea that the peas would fall from his spoon into the hose. The vacuum would suck all the peas up, and they'd be gone forever! Milo figured he could just cough when he turned the vacuum cleaner on so that no one could hear the noise. Milo couldn't wait to try out his machine. He knew he had a perfect plan.

The next day, Milo raced home from school to try his invention. No one else was home. Milo heated some peas in the microwave oven. Then he put them on a dish.

Milo set up his invention. He sat down and picked up some peas with his spoon. The peas went down the hose, but they got stuck and came back out! There was no one to turn on the vacuum cleaner, so the **experiment** didn't work. Milo had to solve this new problem.

Name _____ Date _____

　　Milo decided he needed someone to help turn on the vacuum cleaner. He needed someone he could trust. He thought about Anne and Ed but decided they would tell on him. Then he remembered Jenna, his friend who lived next door. Jenna hated peas, too. They could set up a signal, and she could turn the machine on. Milo thought he had a grand plan!

　　Milo talked to Jenna. She said she would help. Jenna would turn on the vacuum cleaner just after Milo's mom sat down.

　　That night, Milo sat down at the dinner table. He looked out the window. Jenna waved. Mom put peas in front of him. He took a big helping and put some on his spoon. Then Mom sat down.

　　Suddenly there was a huge noise. Then the peas disappeared from Milo's plate. It worked! Everyone stared at Milo.

　　Dad said, "What in the world is that?"

　　Milo said, "It's my invention called Milo's Peas-Be-Gone! It gets rid of peas."

　　"If you don't like peas, why didn't you just say so?" asked Mom. "I know another way you can try them. Put some peas on your mashed potatoes."

　　He tried it. He liked it! Milo decided to save his invention. He might need it if Mom ever served **liver.**

Name _____   Date _____

✓ Reading Comprehension Check

Circle the letter next to the **best** answer.

1. What is Milo's problem?
   A Milo's sister likes peas.
   B Milo hates peas.
   C Milo has to vacuum the kitchen.
   D Milo's friend will not help Milo's mom.

2. How does Milo plan to solve his problem?
   A He plans to invent a shirt that will hide all the peas on his plate.
   B He plans to invent a new type of microwave oven.
   C He plans to invent a machine to make peas disappear.
   D He plans to invent a machine to cook tasty peas.

3. Who helps Milo with his plan?
   A Anne and Snap
   B Ed and Anne
   C Ed and Jenna
   D Mom and Jenna

4. Which of the following is an opinion?
   A Peas taste terrible.
   B Peas are green.
   C Peas roll around.
   D Ed loves peas.

Answer the questions below in complete sentences.

5. What steps does Milo take to create his invention? Describe the steps.

   _____
   _____
   _____

6. What should Milo have done before he made his invention?

   _____

Name _____ Date _____

✏️ Vocabulary Practice

Write the vocabulary word from the box that fits each clue to finish the puzzle.

| disappear | basement | create | experiment |
| invention | hose | liver | frozen |

Across

2. a test to find out if something works
4. a room of the house that is under the ground; means the same as "cellar"
5. a long thing that water or air goes through
6. means the same as "make"
7. a kind of meat; rhymes with "river"
8. what something is after you make it very, very cold

Down

1. means the opposite of "to show up"
3. a machine or other thing that has been thought up

Name _____ Date _____

💡 Critical Thinking Activity

1. What is the story's setting? (*Setting* means where and when the story takes place.) Who are the characters? What is Milo's problem? What is his solution? (*Solution* means how a problem is solved.) Use a copy of the Cluster Story Map on page 93 to answer these questions.

2. Milo invented a Peas-Be-Gone machine. What machine would you like to invent? What would the machine do? How would it work? Complete the sentences. Then draw a picture of your machine in the box. You can label the parts of your machine if you want to.

The name of the machine I would like to invent is _____
_____.

My machine would _____
_____
_____.

My machine would work _____
_____
_____
_____.

Picture of my machine

Name _____   Date _____

Get Ready to Read

Suppose you can paint a large blank wall in your school. It tells the story of your community. What do you draw? In this story, children paint a wall to celebrate the school's anniversary. You will read how a community shares in painting the wall.

The School Mural

One morning, Mrs. Ramos greeted her class. "I have some news. Soon our school will be fifty years old. We're going to have an open house on May twenty-fifth to celebrate this big event."

Mrs. Ramos said, "Each class will make a big **project.** It should be about our school and our **community.**"

Paul asked, "What should we do?"

"I'm sure you'll think of some good ideas," said Mrs. Ramos.

The children went outside for recess. Mei Lee and Paul raced for the swings. They liked to see who could swing the highest.

Mei Lee thought about the big project. She said, "I think we should write a song or put on a play for our class project. What do you think?"

Paul said, "We've done those things before. We need a really big project."

While Mei Lee was swinging very high, she looked past the school. She saw the building across the street. It had a big mural painted on the front wall. This gave her a great idea.

Name _____ Date _____

    Later that day, Mrs. Ramos asked the children for their ideas. Paul wanted to print a huge **banner** on the computer. Maria wanted to make bookmarks to give away. Edwina's idea was to make a huge card and have everyone sign it. Mei Lee said, "Let's make a mural."

    "What's a mural?" asked Ted.

    "It's a big picture painted on the wall of a building," said Mei Lee. "Look at this one at the pet shop." She pointed out the window.

    Mrs. Ramos listed the children's ideas on the board. "These are all good ideas," said Mrs. Ramos. "Let's pick one that everyone can have a part in. Look over the list again. Then we'll vote on our project."

    Mrs. Ramos pointed to each idea as they voted. Then she pointed to the mural idea. Sixteen children raised their hands!

    "I think you picked a fine project that everyone can work on," said Mrs. Ramos.

    Mrs. Ramos said, "People from many different **cultures** have painted on walls. Long ago, cave people painted on the walls of their caves. Their paintings tell us how people lived then. Here is a picture of a cave painting. It is a kind of mural." She held up the picture.

    "Murals are huge! We'll need to think of lots of things to show," said Maria.

    Mrs. Ramos said, "Murals tell about people and their community. Think of some things to tell about your school."

    "Let's tell people about our school band," said Beto.

Name _____   Date _____

"We'll need a really big wall for our mural," said Maria.

"What about the outside wall we see when we swing on the playground?" asked Paul. "All the classes see it every day!"

Mrs. Ramos said, "I'll ask our principal, Mr. Park, if it's OK. Mei Lee, since the mural was your idea, please go with me to see him."

Later Mrs. Ramos said, "The principal likes the idea of painting a mural on the wall. He said he will ask if the **local** newspaper will take a picture of the mural. That would show how our community works together."

Beto asked, "Where will we get the paint? We'll need lots of brushes, too."

Paul said, "Let's ask the art teacher for help. Maybe we could ask our families to help us, too. My mom loves to paint."

"Good idea. Please tell your families about our project, and then I'll call them," said Mrs. Ramos.

For the next three weeks, the children worked on the mural. First they planned the scenes to draw. Next the art teacher helped the children draw sketches of the different scenes on the wall.

Then they started painting the mural. Twenty children couldn't all paint at once, so they took turns. First the band group painted. Then the next group painted. Some parents helped paint the high parts of the wall near the roof. It was hard work, but everyone had fun.

Some funny things happened. One day Paul bumped the paint tray and got paint all over himself. Then he slipped and put his hands on the wall. He left his handprints on the mural! Everyone decided it looked good, so they added their handprints, too.

Another time, Angelina was painting high up on a ladder. She dipped the brush into the bucket and splattered lots of paint onto the wall. But down below her was Beto, so she splattered him, too! He had green hair that day.

When the mural was finished, Mr. Park called the newspaper. A **reporter** came to write a story. He asked the children many questions about how they made the mural. He wrote down everyone's name. He took photos of the mural with the painters in front of it. He told the children to watch for the **article** soon.

Name _____ Date _____

The children could hardly wait to see the article in the newspaper. After about a week, the article appeared with a big photo of the mural. The headline said, "Children Show School Pride."

On the day of the open house, Mr. Park spoke to all the children, parents, and visitors. He told everyone what project each class had done. Then he invited the visitors to walk around and see all the projects. The children were very proud and excited.

When Mr. Park told about the mural, the crowd cheered. One neighbor stood up and thanked the children for making such a beautiful painting. He said people would enjoy it for many years.

The newspaper reporter came again, too. He took more pictures of the mural and the children.

Some of the children decided they liked painting so much that it became their new **hobby.** Someday they might be famous painters. Or maybe they'll come back to the school sometime just to enjoy their mural. They might even tell children at the school the story of how their mural came to be.

Name _____ Date _____

✓ Reading Comprehension Check

Fill in the circle next to the **best** answer.

1. Which of these things happens first?
   - A The students sketch scenes for the mural on the wall.
   - B Mrs. Ramos tells parents about the mural project.
   - C The art teacher helps students plan the scenes for the mural.
   - D The students put their handprints on the wall.

2. Who does NOT help paint or plan the mural?
   - A the principal
   - B students
   - C the art teacher
   - D parents

3. Because of the mural project, some of the students—
   - A go back to see the mural when they are older.
   - B write an article about painting the mural.
   - C become famous painters.
   - D start painting as a hobby.

4. The author most likely wrote "The School Mural" to—
   - A teach readers how to paint a mural.
   - B tell an interesting story about a mural.
   - C show why painting a mural is a good idea.
   - D explain what murals are.

Answer the questions below in complete sentences.

5. *Pride* is what you show when you are proud of something. Why do you think the reporter uses "Children Show School Pride" as the headline of his newspaper article?

_____

_____

6. Name one fact about murals that you learned from the story.

_____

_____

Name _____ Date _____

✏️ Vocabulary Practice

Write the words from the box to complete the paragraphs.

| community | article | banner | hobby |
| cultures | project | reporter | local |

Laura loved to paint. It was her favorite (**1.**) _____.
One summer day Laura saw a (**2.**) _____ hanging over a street downtown. It said "Our (**3.**) _____ needs a mural. Come help." Laura wanted to help her town by working on this (**4.**) _____. So for two weeks she helped paint the mural.

The mural showed people from the many different (**5.**) _____ who lived in the town. One of the painters called the (**6.**) _____ newspaper. She said, "We think an (**7.**) _____ about the mural should be in the newspaper. Please send a (**8.**) _____ who can write about it." A few days later, Laura read all about her work in the newspaper.

✏️ Vocabulary Extension

Choose two vocabulary words. Describe something that is an example and something that is not an example for each word.

Word:	Word:
Example:	Example:
Non-example:	Non-example:

Name _____ Date _____

💡 Critical Thinking Activity

1. What is the cause of each of the following events in the story?

   Mei Lee wants the children to paint a mural for their project.
   Mrs. Ramos and Mei Lee talk to the principal.
   All the children add their handprints to the mural.

   Use a copy of the Cause and Effect Chart on page 88. Write each event in the EFFECT column. Then write the cause of each effect, or event, in the CAUSE column

2. Name three things you would paint in a mural for your school or community. Draw a picture in the box of one part of the mural.

   _____

   _____

EXTRA: Find a picture of a mural in a book or on the Internet. Look at it carefully. What were the painters of this mural proud of?

Name _____   Date _____

Get Ready to Read

You may have read history books about pioneers. What do you remember about the dangers they faced? Have you ever wondered what it would be like to live during that time? Read on to learn about the adventures of one pioneer boy.

Diary of a Pioneer Boy

April 28, 1885

My name is Ben Wilkins. I live in St. Louis, Missouri. I will not live here for much longer, though. We are moving! My mother got me a little book and some pencils so I could write about our move and our new life.

Last night I lay awake in my bed. My mother and father were in the kitchen. I could hear them talking to each other.

"I can no longer make a good living in this city. It's time to go west," my father said to my mother.

My heart began to flutter. My older brother, Conrad, whispered, "Father wants us to move!"

"Andrew," said my mother, "I know it has been hard to find work lately. I think you are right. It would be good for us to make a new start."

"Yes," said Father, "it is time to move on. More families have moved here. Many of the men are carpenters, too. Soon I will be out of work."

Name _____ Date _____

    I think my parents knew we could hear them because they began to whisper. The only thing I heard them say after that was "Montana."

    My older brother, Conrad, grumbled into his pillow. My sister, Sarah, came in from her room. "I don't want to leave here," she said. "I don't want to leave my friends!" Gabriel, the baby, made a little crying sound in his crib.

    Montana. I don't know much about it, but I like the sound of it. My sister and older brother don't want to leave St. Louis, but I do. I want to go somewhere I've never been. I want to be an explorer. I want an adventure!

June 8, 1885

    For six long days we have ridden down winding roads and along a big river. We sleep in the wagon every night.

    Conrad and Father were hunting for squirrels this morning, but Father wouldn't let me go. He says I am too young. I do not like being treated like a baby! Someday they will see I am smart and quick!

September 6, 1885

    After fourteen weeks in the wagon, we have finally arrived in Montana. Father bought some land to build a ranch and raise cattle. He and Conrad built a small barn for the animals and a little lean-to for us. Winter comes early in Montana, so we must finish our cabin soon.

Name _____ Date _____

September 8, 1885

   Mother and Sarah have finished planting our garden. They have tied bits of tin on strings to keep the birds away. I must do my chores. Father and Conrad left early this morning. They are going into town to buy supplies and several head of cattle.

September 10, 1885

   This morning Mother sent me to the creek to get reeds for her. I was so busy having fun that I didn't notice the day had grown misty, dark, and cool. I could no longer tell which way was south. At first I thought it didn't matter. I could find our cabin by following the creek. I climbed back onto my horse Scout. At that moment, one of the creek snakes **slithered** by Scout's foot. Scout took off in a gallop.

   I yelled for him to stop. I pulled back on the reins as hard as I could. We reached a **gully,** and Scout leaped over it. I fell off and hit the dirt. Scout was gone. I knew I was truly lost.

   I walked for a long time. I must have walked for miles. Then I heard a strange noise. It turned out to be someone in a wagon. The person was so **bundled** up that I thought it was a scarecrow. I ducked down and held still. The scarecrow climbed down and asked what I was doing all alone.

   I **realized** it wasn't a scarecrow after all. It was a woman as old as Grandmother Wilkins back in St. Louis. She had cracked lips, dark skin, and wrinkles across her cheeks. She wore a man's jacket and trousers.

Name _____ Date _____

She asked me if I wanted to stay with her until the fog lifted. I said yes. I really didn't have any choice.

The woman and I sat in the fog and waited for it to lift. She lit a fire and made coffee. Then we talked. She said she was Mary Fields. She was born in 1832 on the Dunn family farm in Tennessee. When the Civil War was over, Mary left the Dunns.

Mary told me that she needed to go west to find adventure. I explained that I had come west for the same reason.

Mary goes back and forth between town and the mission driving a wagon. She picks up supplies in town and takes them to the mission. This is what she was doing when the fog came in.

I noticed that the fog was gone. I didn't want Mary to know I was lost, but I really didn't know how to get back home. I finally had to tell her. Mary agreed to let me ride with her but explained that she was already late getting to the mission and that we'd have to go there first.

We rode along a bumpy trail toward the mountain. I knew my family must be worried, but I didn't have a choice.

Then I noticed a bear was following us. The old bear was snorting and trotting along just yards behind us. He looked very hungry. I wasn't going to wait for him to jump in the wagon. I hopped in the back, picked up two of Mary's pans, and smacked them together. The bear grunted and waddled off. Mary told me she couldn't have done it better herself.

www.harcourtschoolsupply.com
© HMH Supplemental Publishers Inc. All rights reserved.

Lesson 12: Diary of a Pioneer Boy
Leveled Reading: Realistic Fiction, SV 9781419099632

Name _____ Date _____

When we reached the top of the mountain ridge, Mary pulled the horses to a stop. She sniffed the air and quickly drove the wagon behind some thick spruce trees. Mary looked worried. Then I heard horses' hooves and men's voices. Mary whispered that they were outlaws.

I knew about outlaws. They stole gold and horses. They were bad.

The men stopped their horses on the other side of the trees. One man got down to stretch his legs. He looked all around as he walked. The other outlaw slid down off his horse.

Mary looked frightened. I grabbed a hammer from the wagon and threw it as far as I could. It landed with a crash in some weeds.

The outlaws decided it must have been a **critter** and left. Mary smiled a big smile. We decided we had had enough adventure for the day.

We finally reached the mission after dark. Several women and children came out to help unload the supplies. I helped, too. They didn't tell me to carry the little things like Father does.

Later we all sat down to supper in a building they call the main hall. Mary and I ate with the children, the women, and some men who helped. Food had never tasted so good in all my life.

I had many adventures today. But I miss my family, and I am tired.

September 11, 1885

I explored the mission this morning. The last place I went was the hospital. I met a very sick girl named Suzanne. I tried to make Suzanne feel better by drawing a picture with her. I let her keep my pencil.

When Mary called me, I told Suzanne goodbye. Outside the hospital, Mary and I waved goodbye to the people of St. Peter's Mission. We drove out across the field to the hills. Mary and I drove the horses for hours, back across the mountains and down the grassy plains. It was late in the afternoon when we saw my ranch. I jumped from Mary's wagon and ran all the way to the door. My mother met me and hugged me so hard I could hardly breathe. She told me she had been very worried and that she shouldn't have asked me to go off to do such a dangerous chore.

Mary told my parents about our adventures and about how I had chased away a bear and tricked the outlaws. She told them I was a fine young man.

Just at that moment, I remembered I had lost Scout. My father told me he had found his way home before I did. I was so happy!

At bedtime, my father told me he knew I was not a little boy anymore. I am lots of things. I am grown up. I am a pioneer. I am an explorer. But best of all, at least for now, I am home.

Name _____ Date _____

✓ Reading Comprehension Check

Complete each sentence below. Use what you read in the passage.

1. Ben Wilkins and his family move from Missouri to _____
   _____.

2. Ben is excited about the move because _____
   _____.

3. Ben gets lost when _____
   _____.

4. Because Ben gets lost, he _____
   _____.

5. Mary's job is to _____
   _____.

6. From the details given about Mary Fields's life on page 73, you can infer that she _____
   _____.

7. When Ben and Mary are in the wagon, Ben scares a _____ and outsmarts _____.

8. Mary and Ben are the same because they both _____
   _____.

9. One thing in the story that can happen in real life is _____
   _____.

Name _____ Date _____

✏️ Vocabulary Practice

Choose a word from the box that can take the place of the underlined word or words in the sentence. Write the word on the line.

bundled	critter	realized
gully	slithered	

1. The <u>creek bed</u> was dry because it had not rained for months. _____

2. The little boy was <u>wrapped up</u> in a coat and blankets. _____

3. Some kind of <u>animal</u> is walking near our tent! _____

4. The snake <u>slid</u> across the desert sand. _____

5. When Celia did badly on the test, she <u>understood</u> that she should have studied more. _____

✏️ Vocabulary Extension

Choose your favorite vocabulary word. Write it in the chart below. Then write what the word means in your own words. Draw a picture to illustrate the word and help you remember it in the future.

Word:	
Definition in my own words:	
Illustration:	

Name _____ Date _____

💡 Critical Thinking Activity

1. How does your life compare and contrast with Ben's life? Use a copy of the Compare and Contrast Chart on page 92 to answer this question.

2. Write a review of the story in the form of a diary entry. Begin with *Dear Diary, Today I read a story about . . . .* Write what you like and don't like about the story. Then read or explain your diary entry to a partner.

_____
_____
_____
_____
_____
_____
_____
_____
_____
_____
_____
_____
_____

Name _____   Date _____

> **Get Ready to Read**
>
> In which state is the Grand Canyon located? Have you or someone you know traveled there? What words can be used to describe the Grand Canyon? Read on to find out about a girl who travels there and how she shows courage during her trip.

The Grand Canyon Doesn't Scare Me

My parents made plans for me to visit Grandpa and Grandma in Jerome, Arizona, last summer. I was happy when Mom told me. Then I asked Mom how I was going to get there. When she said, "On an airplane," I was less than **thrilled.** I had never been on an airplane before, and I was afraid. After Lizzie Lopat started talking to me about my trip, I was even more afraid.

Lizzie Lopat is weird. She is always sure that things will go wrong. Because she's so sure, she thinks it's foolish to try new things.

"An airplane by yourself?" she asked. "Flying is scary. The plane is too high up in the sky! You'll get sick when it bounces in the air, or you'll get lost in the airport and wind up in Russia!"

That's Lizzie Lopat. She worries so much that her worries have wrinkles. I know the best thing to do is ignore her. Still, by the time I walked onto the plane, I was **terrified.**

After I sat down, a flight attendant sat down in the seat next to me. "Hi," she said. "I'm Carla Johnson. What's your name?"

Name _____ Date _____

"I'm Beth Nevarez," I croaked. "This is the first time I've flown."

"That's great. You must be excited," said Carla.

"I am," I said slowly, "but I'm also scared."

Carla asked why, so I told her about Lizzie and all the things she told me. I hadn't told anyone about Lizzie's crazy worries before. I'm not sure why I did then. But Carla did something that was perfect. She talked about each of the things Lizzie had said and why I shouldn't worry about them. In just a few minutes, she really helped me to relax. Then Carla had to get ready for the flight.

When the plane lifted into the air, I realized something. Lizzie would never be brave enough to fly in an airplane. I knew that was one reason I'm tougher than Lizzie Lopat.

After we landed in Phoenix, Carla took me to meet my grandparents at the gate. When I saw them, I thanked Carla for helping me. Then I ran to Grandpa and Grandma and gave them each a big hug.

Our plan was to drive to Jerome, the town where my grandparents live. We would spend a few days there and then head to the Grand Canyon. I couldn't wait!

Jerome is a special town for a couple of reasons, and one isn't good. Jerome sits high on a mountainside. Part of the town once slid down the mountain! Lizzie found out about this before I left Chicago. When she did, she was sure even if I made it to Jerome safely, I would come back down the mountain in one horrible, sliding crash.

Name _____ Date _____

    Our drive to Jerome **involved** many sharp turns on the edges of cliffs. I was really nervous. I guess it would be easy for a car to **plunge** over one of the cliffs on the highway, but Grandma said that the safety record for the highway is better than most flat, straight highways. Grandpa said that people must drive slowly and carefully. I relaxed when Grandpa said this. Unlike Lizzie would have done, I enjoyed the beautiful views as we climbed up the mountain road. That's the second reason I'm tougher than Lizzie Lopat.

    When we arrived in Jerome, we went straight to my grandparents' store. They own a jewelry store that's unlike any other jewelry store. It has a huge back wall of windows with views of the mountains and valleys. Their store is three stories high, and my grandparents live above the store in the top two stories.

    We spent the next few days exploring the town. We took a four-hour **scenic** railroad ride along the mountainside. We rode along the edges of the cliffs, through a long tunnel under the mountain, and over wooden bridges that cross high above water and valleys of rocks and trees. Sometimes I looked out the window to see how far up we were. Once or twice, I was so afraid I had to close my eyes—but not for too long. The beauty of the reddish brown cliffs, the green forest, and the rushing blue river was too good to miss. Of course, Lizzie Lopat wouldn't even be able to look at photos from this kind of trip. She would never even be brave enough to sit on the train. That's the third reason why I'm tougher than she is.

Name _____ Date _____

After our few days in Jerome, we drove north to the Grand Canyon. That's where I learned that sometimes there are very good reasons to be afraid.

We arrived just as the sun was rising at the Grand Canyon. We would hike Bright Angel Trail all the way down the Grand Canyon, camp there overnight, and hike back up the next day.

I relaxed on the trail, but I was only relaxed about hiking. Worries about camping at the bottom of the canyon played in the back of my mind. When we arrived at the campsite, I started thinking about spiders crawling on me while I slept. Then I moved on to worrying about wild animals getting our food or us.

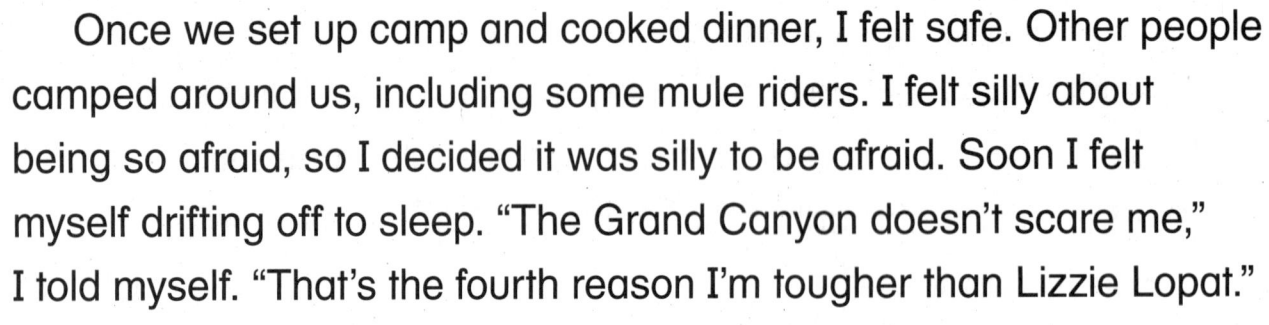

Once we set up camp and cooked dinner, I felt safe. Other people camped around us, including some mule riders. I felt silly about being so afraid, so I decided it was silly to be afraid. Soon I felt myself drifting off to sleep. "The Grand Canyon doesn't scare me," I told myself. "That's the fourth reason I'm tougher than Lizzie Lopat."

The next morning, we ate early and started to hike up Bright Angel Trail. It was difficult at first, but after two hours of climbing, I felt good. Suddenly everything changed. I heard a noise. Right before my eyes, Grandpa slipped and fell feet-first over the side of the cliff!

Grandma and I moved as quickly and carefully as possible to the edge of the cliff. We looked over and got a wonderful surprise. Grandpa was sitting on a rock a few feet below us. When he saw us, he said, "Be careful. I just noticed that it's slippery up there."

When Grandpa stood up, he couldn't stand on his ankle. It was clear that he wasn't going to hike anymore that day.

We helped Grandpa move to a shady spot near the trail. Grandma did a little first aid on Grandpa's scratches and ankle. As Grandma worked, we heard a clopping sound from down the trail. It came closer. We saw the mule riders from our campsite climbing back up.

Eventually the mule riders made their way up to us and stopped when they saw us. The guides in charge looked at Grandpa's ankle. They were trained in first aid and both thought it was a bad **sprain.** They also thought the best thing for us to do was ride up to the top of the trail with them. Worse than that, they said we would ride two to a mule. They said this as if it were no big deal.

Grandma patted me and whispered, "Don't worry. The mules can handle this." I don't know how people can always tell when I'm afraid.

The guides decided that each one of them would take an extra rider. Grandpa would ride with the male guide and Grandma with the female. Then they pointed to a young boy. The guide said, "Your partner is Brendan. He's turning out to be a mule expert. You'll both be fine."

Brendan said to me, "I was a little scared yesterday, but Old Surefoot is a good mule. If he weren't, they wouldn't put two kids on him. Don't worry."

The mules in front of us started climbing up the trail. I held on to Brendan's waist tightly. After we traveled over several narrow trails, I thought about Lizzie for the first time that day. Of course, she wouldn't ride a mule. She'd be **paralyzed** with fear. But here I was riding Old Surefoot up a narrow Grand Canyon trail. That's the fifth reason why I'm tougher than Lizzie Lopat.

In a few hours, we were at the top of the trail. My grandparents and I thanked the mule riders. Then we went to the hospital. The doctor said Grandpa had a broken ankle!

In spite of Grandpa's **injury,** I enjoyed the rest of my Arizona visit. When it ended and I was on the plane back to Chicago, I got a little nervous. But compared to riding Old Surefoot up the Grand Canyon, flying didn't seem scary after all.

Guess who was the flight attendant? Carla Johnson! I told her about my trip. She said, "I'll bet you can't wait to tell Lizzie about Arizona."

I had forgotten that I had told Carla about Lizzie. I also realized I hadn't thought about Lizzie since I climbed off Old Surefoot. Then I decided to tell Carla something no one else knew. "Carla, there is no Lizzie Lopat. She was me. My name is Elizabeth Lopat Nevarez. *Lizzie* and *Beth* are both nicknames for *Elizabeth.* Lizzie was the part of me that was always afraid. Beth is, well, me."

Carla smiled and said, "It sounds like Lizzie isn't flying back to Chicago with you."

It was true. Somehow I had said goodbye to Lizzie on Bright Angel Trail. I would always have fears. Everyone does. But I wouldn't let my fears make my decisions. And that's the sixth reason why I'm tougher than Lizzie Lopat!

Six Reasons Why I'm Tougher Than Lizzie Lopat

1. I flew in an airplane.
2. I rode in a car up a mountain road with dangerous curves.
3. I took a train tour on a mountain railroad.
4. I slept at the bottom of the Grand Canyon.
5. I rode a mule up a narrow Grand Canyon trail.
6. I learned not to give in to my fears.

Name _____ Date _____

✓ Reading Comprehension Check

Circle the letter next to the **best** answer.

1. The setting of the story is—
   A Chicago in the 1800s.
   B Arizona in the 1800s.
   C present-day Arizona.
   D present-day Chicago.

2. Elizabeth is afraid of flying because—
   A her friends have told her scary stories.
   B she has never been on an airplane before.
   C her grandparents will meet her at the airport.
   D she gets sick when she is on an airplane.

3. Elizabeth feels better about flying after she talks to—
   A Lizzie.
   B Grandma.
   C Carla.
   D Brendan.

4. The author most likely wrote this story to—
   A persuade readers to try mountain climbing.
   B entertain readers with a mystery about a family who finds treasure.
   C persuade readers to travel to the landforms in Arizona.
   D entertain readers with a story about someone who overcomes fears.

Answer the questions below in complete sentences.

5. Beth says, "But I wouldn't let my fears make my decisions." Based on this statement, do you think Beth is likely to go on another adventure? Explain your answer.

   _____

   _____

6. Use your own words to tell what this story is about.

   _____

   _____

Name _____ Date _____

✎ Vocabulary Practice

Choose a word from the box to complete each sentence. Write each word on the line.

| injury | scenic | eventually | terrified | sprain |
| involved | paralyzed | thrilled | plunge | |

1. The opposite of *not excited* is _____.

2. Someone who has an _____ has been hurt.

3. To _____ means "to go down suddenly."

4. A person who is _____ cannot move.

5. The opposite of *brave* is _____.

6. A word that means almost the same as *included* is _____.

7. A person with a _____ has badly twisted a muscle.

8. The word _____ means "having to do with the scenes around you."

9. A word that means almost the same as *finally* is _____.

✎ Vocabulary Extension

Choose your favorite vocabulary word. Complete the graphic organizer.

Word:
Looks like:
Sounds like:
Feels like:
Synonym:

Name _____ Date _____

💡 Critical Thinking Activity

1. How does Beth change in the story? What causes her to change? Use a copy of the Character Change Story Map on page 89 to answer these questions.

2. Complete a copy of the Cause and Effect Chart on page 88 with the following causes and effects. Write each one in a different row of the chart. Then complete the chart by writing the effect or cause for each item.

   CAUSE: Beth talks to Carla on the flight to Arizona.

   CAUSE: Grandpa breaks his ankle.

   EFFECT: Beth is nervous during the drive to Jerome.

   EFFECT: Beth is worried at the campsite.

   EFFECT: Beth says goodbye to Lizzie Lopat.

3. Imagine that you are Beth. You are now back home after your visit (and your adventure!) with your grandparents. Write a letter on a separate sheet of paper to a good friend telling about your visit. In your letter tell about the lesson or lessons you learned.

4. How are you like Beth? How are you different? On the lines below compare yourself to Beth.

   _____
   _____
   _____
   _____

EXTRA: Even though Lizzie Lopat and Elizabeth Lopat Nevarez are the same person, they are very different. Write a list of their differences.

Name _____ Date _____

Cause and Effect Chart

Title _____

Cause	Effect

Name _____ Date _____

Character Change Story Map

Title _____

Character _____

Character at Beginning	Events That Cause Change	Character at End

Name _____ Date _____

Character Traits Web

Trait
Example

Trait
Example

Character

Trait
Example

Trait
Example

Name _____ Date _____

Story Events Map

Title _____

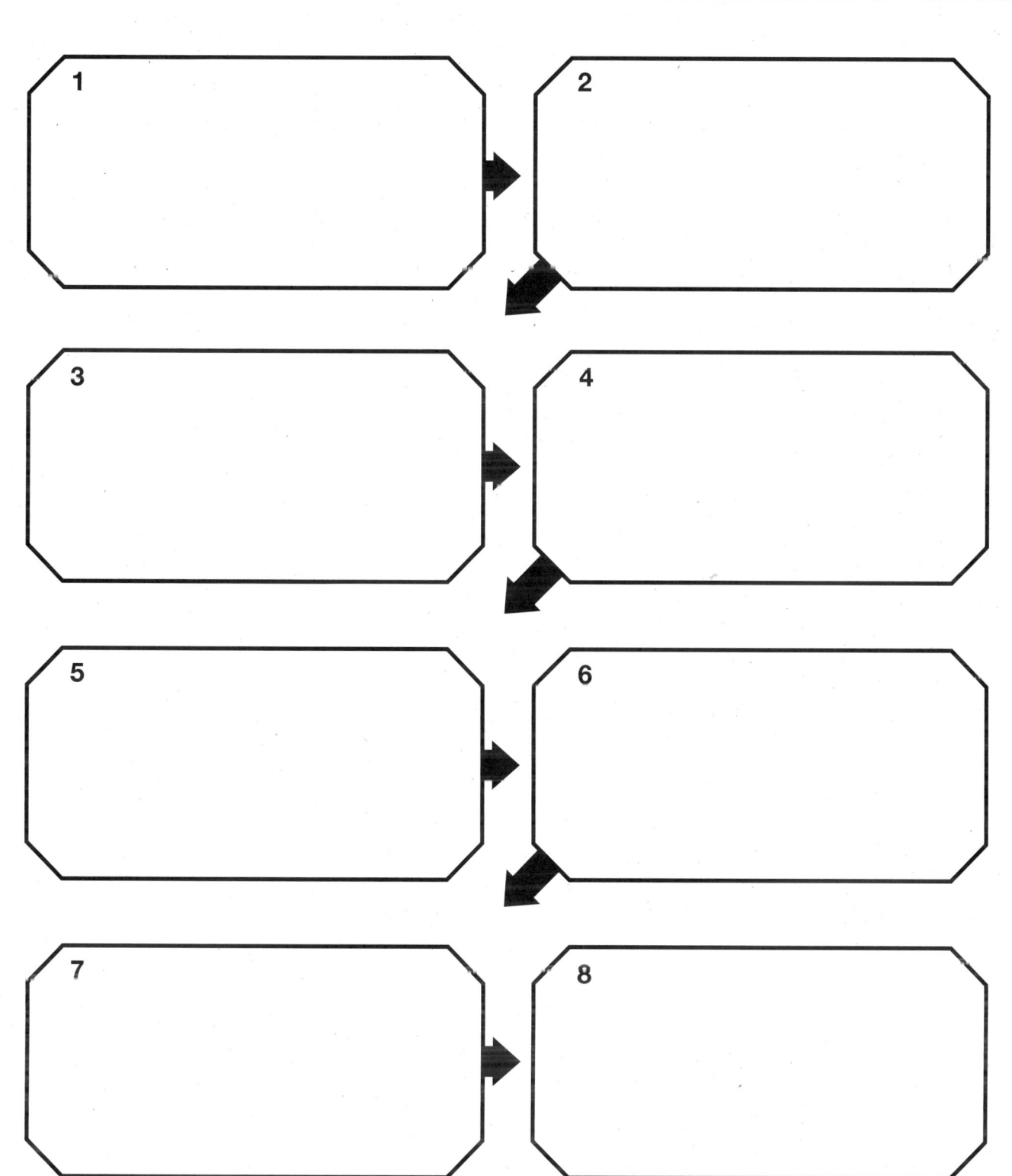

1	2
3	4
5	6
7	8

Name _____   Date _____

Compare and Contrast Chart

Title _____

Topics

Compare (Alike)

Contrast (Different)

Name _____ Date _____

Cluster Story Map

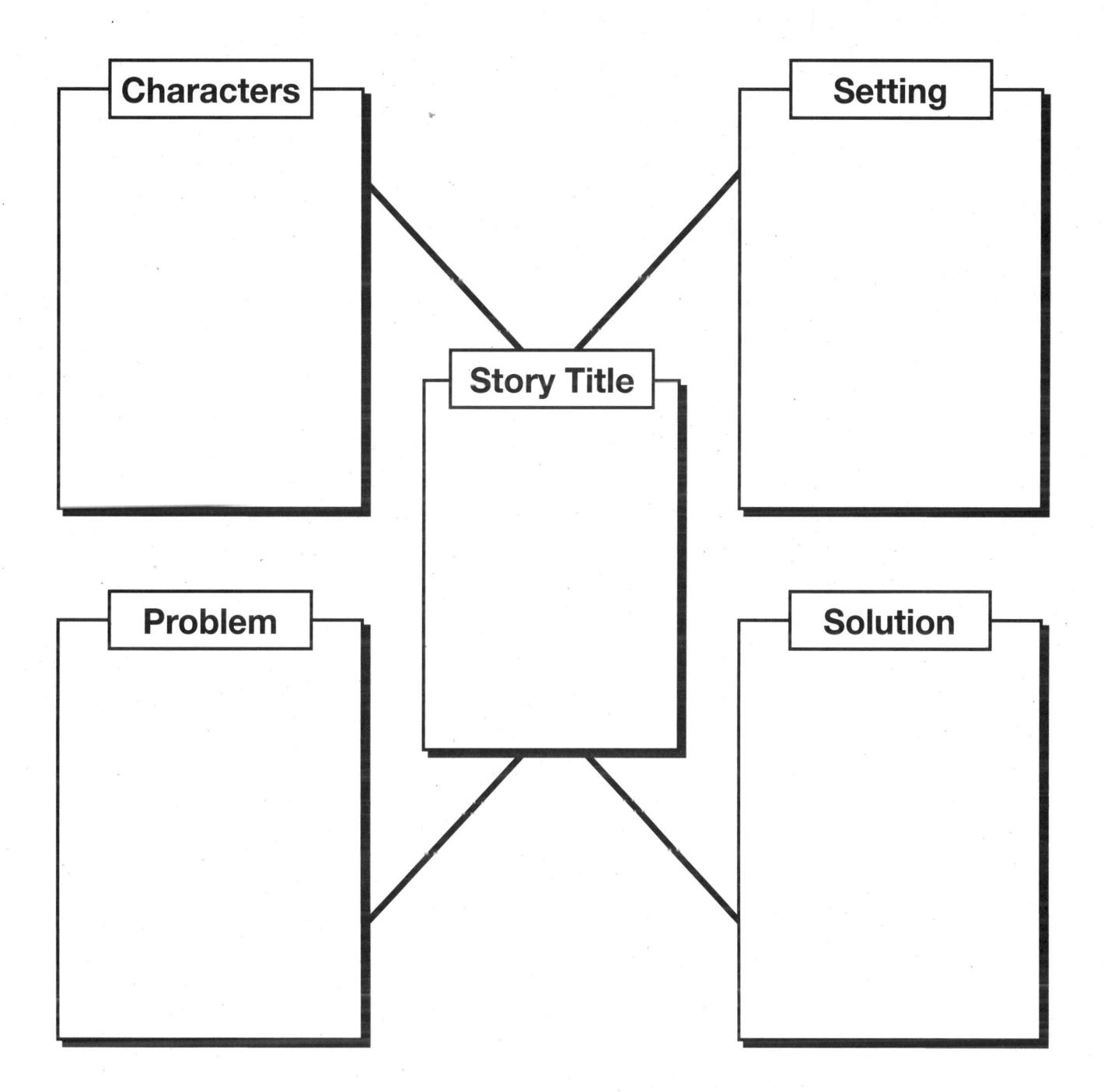

Characters

Setting

Story Title

Problem

Solution

Answer Key

Page 7
1. A
2. C
3. D
4. B
5. This story is mostly about a child and grandmother who make music together.
6. Sample answer: The writer and grandmother have a close relationship. They do fun things together.

Page 8
1. star
2. howl
3. whistle
4. together
5. concert

Pictures will vary.

Page 9
1. Answers will vary.
2. Pictures will vary.

Page 12
1. the zoo
2. he went to school without his lunchbox
3. monkeys; elephants
4. Answers will vary.
5. he cannot find his backpack
6. take the lunchbox to Benny
7. eat his lunch at the zoo
8. Sample answer: entertain readers with a story that could really happen

Page 13
Across
3. cried
5. remembered
6. lunchbox
Down
1. wondered
2. driver
4. forgot

Page 14
1.–4. Answers will vary.
Sample answers:
(1) Benny's dad took Benny his lunchbox at school. (2) Benny's teacher took Benny his lunchbox on the bus. (3) The bus driver took Benny his lunchbox at the zoo. (4) At lunchtime Benny could not find his lunchbox. (5) Benny saw a monkey eating a banana that might be his. (6) Benny saw an elephant eating peanuts that might be his. (7) Benny remembered that his lunchbox was in his backpack. (8) Benny's teacher told Benny his backpack was on his back.

Page 17
1. vet
2. turn; spin
3. pilot
4. concerts
5. astronaut
6. stage
7. dentist
8. stories

Page 18
1. B
2. A
3. D
4. D

Answers will vary.

Page 19
1.–3. Answers will vary.

Page 22
1. Nikki is frowning because she isn't having a very good day.
2. Nikki finds 41¢.
3. Sample answer: Grandpa is a positive person. He tells Nikki that they can turn her "frown upside down."
4. Nikki and Grandpa stop at the bakery.
5. If Nikki's luck continues, she will most likely find more money at the bakery.
6. Sample answer: Because Nikki finds the penny, she has a lucky day. Her bad day turns into a great day.

Page 23
1. bookshelf
2. frown
3. nickel
4. dime
5. bin
6. shiny
7. quarter
8. coin

Page 24
1. Answers will vary but should mention events from the story.
2. Title: A Penny Changes the Day
Character: Nikki
Sample answers:
Character at Beginning: Nikki is sad.
Events That Cause Change: Nikki finds a nickel in a bin of nails; Nikki finds a dime under a bookshelf; Nikki finds a quarter in a chair.
Character at End: Nikki is happy.

Page 27
1. C
2. D
3. A
4. B
5. John Claude opens an egg the right way.
6. Sample answer: A boy makes egg nests with his grandmother.

Page 28
1. spatula
2. sizzle
3. poured
4. rim
5. gathered
6. special
7. splattered
8. gently

Answers will vary.

Page 29
1. Step One: Gather a spatula, special pan, glass, fork, cup, bread, and eggs.
Step Two: Use the glass to cut holes in the bread.
Step Three: Crack an egg into a cup.
Step Four: Put bread in the pan and let it brown.
Step Five: Beat the eggs.
Step Six: Pour eggs into the bread holes and let them cook.
2. Answers will vary.

Page 32
1. C
2. B
3. C
4. D
5. Sample answer: Pepito does enjoy his Cuban sandwich when he eats it. He says "Mmmm" in the story.
6. Answers will vary.

Page 33
1. crunchy
2. lunchtime
3. sandwich
4. tastes

Answers will vary.

Page 34
1. Sample answers:
(1) Pepito's aunt makes him a Cuban sandwich. (2) Pepito tells his friends about the sandwich. (3) Lee says that his grandfather cooks wontons for him. (4) Tara says that her aunt cooks plantains for her. (5) Ray says that his father cooks poori for him. (6) Ana says that her mother

cooks buñuelos for her. (7) Pepito eats his sandwich at lunch and says it tastes like a ham and cheese sandwich.
2. Sample answers: plantains, Africa, like a fried banana; poori, India, like fried bread; buñuelos, Mexico, like doughnuts; Cuban sandwich, Cuba, like a ham and cheese sandwich.
3. Thank-you notes will vary.

Page 38
1. D
2. C
3. B
4. A
5. Everything in the story could happen in real life.
6. Sample answer: A boy's friends in the neighborhood help him and his mom when his parrot flies away. When they find the parrot, they see that it has a new friend.

Page 39
1. B
2. A
3. C
4. D
5. B
6. C
Answers will vary.

Page 40
1. Stories will vary but should include a problem that is solved with the help of one or more persons.
2. Maps will vary. Names of places in the story should be labeled, and the order in which the places are mentioned in the story should be ordered as follows: (1) James's house; (2) the sidewalk near James's house where Cassie is playing; (3) farther down the same sidewalk, where Chris is riding a bike; (4) even farther down the same sidewalk, where Anna is roller-skating; (5) Mrs. Chang's house (even farther down the same sidewalk); (6) Mr. Ford's house (even farther down the same sidewalk); (7) the park.

Page 44
1. B
2. A
3. D
4. C
5. B
6. D
7. Answers will vary.

Page 45
1. magazine
2. cousin
3. supplies
4. mail carrier
5. title
6. photos
7. clay
8. except
9. favorite
Pictures will vary.

Page 46
1. Answers will vary.
2. Story Title: A Gift to Share
Characters: Mattie, her brother, her cousin, Mom, Aunt Debra
Problem: Mattie does not know what to give Aunt Debra for her birthday.
Solution: Mattie makes a special book about herself to give Aunt Debra.

Page 52
1. Sample answer: Emma feels very impatient. She wants to get Lucy, but Mom, Dad, and Ty are doing things that will make them get Lucy later.
2. Sample answer: Emma's writing for "June 6, Afternoon" is mostly about Emma meeting Lucy and getting to know her.
3. Sample answer: The storm cloud is tall and wide, just like a giant mountain.
4. Sample answer: Emma does not think Lucy can swim, and she is afraid that Lucy will get in the pond and drown.
5. Sample answer: Emma jumps in the pond and starts swimming after she sees Lucy swimming there.
6. Sample answer: Emma starts to think in a different way about Ty after he shows her how to swim underwater. He had teased her before about not being able to swim.

Page 53
1. strangers
2. protect
3. ducked
4. diary
5. shutters
6. coughing
7. million
8. tongue
9. upset
10. prairie
11. celebrate

Page 54
1. Answers will vary.
2. Diary entries will vary.

Page 59
1. B
2. C
3. C
4. A
5. Answers will vary.
6. Sample answer: Milo should have told his parents that he does not like peas.

Page 60
Across
2. experiment
4. basement
5. hose
6. create
7. liver
8. frozen
Down
1. disappear
3. invention

Page 61
1. Story Title: Milo's Great Invention
Setting: Milo's house
Characters: Milo, Mom, Dad, Ed, Anne, Jenna
Problem: Milo does not like peas and needs to think of a way to get rid of them.
Solution: Milo invents a Peas-Be-Gone machine to get rid of the peas.
2. Answers and drawings will vary.

Page 67
1. B
2. A
3. D
4. B
5. Sample answer: The children have shown that they are proud of their school by working hard to paint a beautiful mural.
6. Sample answers: A mural is a big picture painted on the wall of a building; murals tell about people and their community; a cave painting is a kind of mural.

Page 68
1. hobby
2. banner
3. community
4. project
5. cultures
6. local
7. article
8. reporter
Answers will vary.

Page 69
1. Sample answers:
   CAUSES: (1) Mei Lee sees a mural on a building at recess.
   (2) Mrs. Ramos needs to ask the principal if it is OK to paint the mural.
   (3) Everyone decides that Paul's handprints look good on the wall.
2. Ideas and pictures will vary.

Page 76
1. Montana
2. he wants to go somewhere new
3. he goes to find reeds by the creek for his mother
4. Sample answer: meets Mary Fields and proves he isn't a little boy
5. bring supplies from town to the mission on her wagon
6. Sample answer: was bored living on a farm as a young girl
7. bear; outlaws
8. Sample answer: like to go on adventures
9. Answers will vary.

Page 77
1. gully
2. bundled
3. critter
4. slithered
5. realized

Answers and pictures will vary.

Page 78
1. Answers will vary.
2. Diary entries will vary.

Page 85
1. C
2. B
3. C
4. D
5. Answers will vary.
6. Answers will vary.

Page 86
1. thrilled
2. injury
3. plunge
4. paralyzed
5. terrified
6. involved
7. sprain
8. scenic
9. eventually

Answers will vary.

Page 87
1. Title: The Grand Canyon Doesn't Scare Me
   Character: Beth
   Sample answers:
   Character at Beginning: Beth is scared of everything that is new.
   Events That Cause Change: Beth stops being scared of flying after Carla talks to her. Beth stops being scared of plunging off the highway after Grandpa tells her it is safe. Beth stops worrying about camping when she sees other people camping around her. Beth rides on a mule without feeling scared.
   Character at End: Beth is no longer scared of everything that is new.
2. EFFECT: Beth relaxes and stops being afraid of flying.
   EFFECT: Beth, Grandpa, and Grandma ride mules back to the top of the trail.
   CAUSE: The road has many sharp turns on edges of cliffs.
   CAUSE: Beth thinks about spiders and wild animals.
   CAUSE: Beth is no longer afraid all the time.
3. Letters will vary.
4. Answers will vary.